# Good Essay Writing

## A SOCIAL SCIENCES GUIDE

## PETER REDMAN ET AL.

The Open University

## Project Team

Sue Cole  *Associate Lecturer*
Rosie Collins  *Associate Lecturer*
Jonathan Davies  *Designer*
Rick Davies  *Associate Lecturer*
Peggotty Graham  *Sub-Dean, Social Sciences*
Peter Hull  *Associate Lecturer*
Mary Larkin  *Associate Lecturer*
Helen Lentell  *Staff Tutor, Social Sciences*
Liz Ockleford  *Associate Lecturer*
Peter Redman  *Staff Tutor, Social Sciences*
Isobel Shelton  *Associate Lecturer*
Lynne Slocombe  *Editor*
Andy Sutton  *Associate Lecturer*

Thanks are also due to: Chris Brook, Lecturer in Geography; Ross Fergusson, Staff Tutor, Social Sciences; Chris Nichols, Course Manager; Diane Watson, Staff Tutor, Social Sciences; and Helen Westcott, Lecturer in Psychology.

Details of enrolment as a student on Open University courses are available from Course Enquiries Data Service, PO Box 625, Dane Road, Milton Keynes MK1 1TY; telephone + 44 - (0)1908 858585.

If you have a professional interest in education and training and would like to learn more about the availability and licensing of distance-learning materials produced by The Open University, please contact Open University Worldwide, The Berrill Building, Walton Hall, Milton Keynes MK7 6AA, UK.
Telephone + 44 - (0)1908 858785

The Open University
Walton Hall, Milton Keynes, MK7 6AA

First published by The Open University 1998

ISBN 0 7942 8915 5

Edited, designed and typeset by The Open University.

Printed and bound by Scotprint Ltd., Musselburgh, Scotland.

1.1

# Contents

# *Preface*

Many students, however experienced, find essay writing difficult. Many, particularly those returning to study after a long break, find essay writing daunting. There is no guaranteed recipe for a good essay, no absolute method. What this book does is to recommend and illustrate proven approaches and techniques which, combined with practice, will increase confidence and skill. It is primarily intended for Open University students working on social sciences courses at degree level, but there is a great deal in the book that will be helpful to a much wider audience of students who want to write good essays.

In the early part of the book, characteristics of marking schemes are given in detail to show how marking essays is not a 'woolly' process, and how the characteristics can be related to a list of recognized writing skills to be aimed for. Recommendations on how to approach different types of essay questions are there to be consulted as and when particular questions arise. There are guidelines on the functions and appropriate length of introductions and conclusions, examples of various ways of supporting and sustaining the main arguments, and hints about structure, style and direction in writing. All of these are illustrated with concrete examples and encapsulated in summaries, while a quick glance through the contents list will enable you to find what you need.

Some sections of the book are best used as reference material. There is an appendix on how to interpret 'process' words in essay questions and one on academic abbreviations and their use. Another appendix provides helpful hints on how to use feedback on essays. There are sections on gender and language issues, and on 'common worries'. Full details of how to reference are provided as well as practical advice as to when references are needed.

Throughout the book are examples of good practice, including brainstorming, fragments of essays, and finally an essay developed from its very beginning to the full final version. These all help to show how very rough notes really can be transformed into the clear flowing prose of a well written essay.

*Good Essay Writing* has been prepared for the Social Sciences Faculty of the Open University as a result of a collective effort. It was initiated in the Open University's East Midlands Region by a team of Associate Lecturers. Subsequently, helpful suggestions have been received from a number of people. Thanks are therefore due to Peter Redman as the main author and to Helen Lentell for getting the project off the ground. Sue Cole, Rosie Collins, Rick Davies, Peter Hull, Mary Larkin, Liz Ockleford and Isobel Shelton all contributed to early drafts. Our thanks to them also. Chris Brook, Ross Fergusson, Chris Nichols, Diane Watson and Helen Westcott provided later suggestions, and Andy Sutton authored the appendix 'Using a word processor to write (or grow) an essay'. Thanks to all these as well as Lynne Slocombe who took on the editing and Jonathan Davies who designed this book. Peggotty Graham co-ordinated the project in its final stages and is therefore responsible for all last minute sins of commission or omission.

We hope that you find this *Good Essay Writing* guide useful and that as a result of studying it your essay writing skills will improve.

Good luck with your studies.

***Peggotty Graham,***
on behalf of the project team.

# 1 Introduction

Essay writing is one of the most important things you'll do while studying the social sciences. It's the point where you finally process all the material that you've been reading, where you grapple with the big ideas, and where you say what you've got to say. What's more, essay writing is about communication. Writing is one of the central ways in which the social scientist makes her or his ideas available to the rest of the world and is thus a key tool in the social scientist's trade. This guide is intended to help you build on your essay writing skills and to improve your abilities as a social scientist. It is not intended to, nor could it, provide all the detailed guidance that you may need for each and every course that you study. Nor does it cover more specialized tasks such as project writing, how to handle graphs and tables and so on. For these and other course-specific requirements you should always take note of the course team's advice and guidance. What the guide does do is help you with a range of generic social sciences conventions and skills that you will need for working at different levels of study in the Social Sciences in The Open University (OU), and more generally. In the process we hope that it will provide you with some concrete ideas about how to improve your essay writing skills.

## 1.1 Why we have produced the guide and why you might need it

On a first level (Level 1) OU course, you are taught basic writing skills within the course materials, in tutorials and via your tutor's comments on returned essays. However, on Level 2 and Level 3 courses there is little time to teach more advanced writing skills. Although you will develop many of these for yourself, there may be some skills that you simply don't know about, or you might be left unsure as to exactly what is expected of your essays at a particular level. For example, it may not be entirely clear to you how to write references, what is different about a Level 2 essay compared to an essay at Level 1, or how complex your analysis is meant to be at Level 3. This guide aims to plug some of these gaps for you. It won't give you all the answers. And it certainly cannot tell you how to write a perfect essay every time. However, it is a resource which you can use when you want to know what to do in a range of different circumstances, what you need to do to improve your general technique, and how you go about writing references, how to avoid plagiarism and so on.

## So who is the guide for?

The guide is designed for those who want to know about more advanced social sciences essay writing skills at degree level. It is written primarily for OU students and is likely to be of especial relevance for all post Level 1 OU students studying Social Sciences or related OU courses who want to improve their essay writing skills. However, much of what follows is also applicable to anyone studying social sciences at degree level. Thus, the guide aims to:

- introduce core social sciences essay writing skills and conventions to people who have not studied social sciences courses before;
- recap basic essay writing skills for people who have already done some studies in the social sciences or related areas;
- introduce more advanced essay writing skills, particularly those needed at Levels 2 and 3.

Inevitably, some of the readers of this guide will be familiar with much of the material already. However, some aspects may be new to you, and other parts will help you build on or develop what you already know.

# 1.2   How to use this guide

The sections that follow cover three main aspects of essay writing and afterwards some general points to look out for.

*Sections 2–5* outline in general terms what is expected from your essays at Levels 1, 2 and 3, explore some basic principles of essay writing, and discuss planning, preparation and writing introductions.

*Section 6* looks at writing the main section of an essay, exploring how to structure an argument, how to support your case, and how to communicate your argument effectively.

*Sections 7 and 8* discuss conclusion writing and explain how to compile references.

*Section 9* looks at some common worries that people have about essays.

After a few concluding remarks in *Section 10*, there are several appendices which contain important information about: learning from past essays, 'process and command' words, using 'mind maps', detailed examples of referencing, academic abbreviations and 'foreign' words, and using word processors to write essays.

How can you use the guide most effectively? There are several approaches. You can:

- read it from cover to cover like a book;
- skim read sections that you already know enough about;
- concentrate on the summaries at the end of each main section;
- pinpoint particular issues that are relevant to you and ignore the rest;
- return to it whenever you need to look something up or remind yourself of a particular point.

Alternatively, you can ignore all of these suggestions and adopt your own reading strategy: backwards, upside down … ! The point is that the book is a resource for you to use how and when you want to.

## 1.3 Open and equal: essay writing and equal opportunities

The OU has a written policy committing itself to avoiding discrimination. This means that it has some responsibilities to you. For example, if you have a physical impairment that makes essay writing problematic, the University will attempt to provide you with the skills and tools that will allow you to produce essays on an equal basis with other students. Similarly, extensions are there to provide some flexibility for people whose other commitments may sometimes interrupt their essay writing (details of the rules governing extensions are available in you in the *Student Handbook*, Section 9). Provisions such as these are not there to give you 'special treatment' or 'unfair advantages'; you have a right to them and should make use of them if you need to. In the first instance, ask your tutor for advice. If you have a disability, you may find it helpful to contact your regional office, where there is a person employed to provide such support.

Just as the University has a responsibility to avoid discriminating against you in relation to essay writing, you have some responsibilities to avoid discriminating against other people. This may involve being critical of some of your own ways of thinking. It may also involve taking care with your choice of words, particularly around issues of disability, 'race', gender, and sexuality. Ask your tutor if you are in any doubt or feel you would like more advice.

## 1.4 Where to go for further help

If you feel you want further help with essay writing, your tutor is the best person to advise you. She or he may be able to arrange extra support for you (either a 'special session' or 'telephone tutorial'). You should also check your course materials for advice on essay writing specifically related to the needs of the course. If you did the OU Level 1 Course D103: *Society and Social Science: A Foundation Course* and have *The Good Study Guide* by Andrew Northedge (Northedge, 1990) you could look back at Chapters 5 and 6 of that. Finally, you should think about talking to other students on your course. Many people will be having the same experiences as you, and you may well find that you learn more from sharing these experiences and looking through each other's essays than from any other source. Choose people you feel comfortable working with, discuss forthcoming essays together and swap assignments when they have been marked.

## 1.5 Will the guide tell me everything about essay writing?

We can't transform your essay writing overnight. The truth is that there is no magic formula that will guarantee you a good grade for every essay that you produce. In fact, there is no one 'correct' way to write an essay. The advice in this guide suggests some generally agreed conventions but these are not the only ones available and they do not by themselves add up to a great essay. Your essay writing will improve mainly through your own hard work in thinking things out for yourself, through experience, and through your increasing knowledge of the fields in which you work. 'How to ...' guides like this one are rather like cookery books: they can tell you what the ingredients are, and they can tell you how to mix the ingredients together, but they won't turn you into a world-class chef. Like cooking, essay writing is not something you ever stop learning about. However, it should help you as you become more confident and more creative in your work.

# 2 Marking schemes and writing skills

Students often want to know what they are expected to do to achieve a better grade. Of course, this differs from question to question, from the beginning of a course to the end of a course, and from level to level. Generally speaking, OU essay questions get more demanding as you progress through a course and as you progress on to higher levels. What follows is intended to give you some ideas of the kinds of things that tutors will probably look for when marking essays.

### Health warning

We have included this section to give you a *broad indication of what may be expected, in general, for different grades.* Remember that individual courses will have their own course-specific requirements for each of the grade ranges, and also that the requirements will vary depending on whether the course is at Level 1, Level 2 or Level 3. In addition, it is important to remember that grading an essay is always a matter of weighing up not only the structure, content and style of the essay, but the interplay between these, together with the interplay between any number of the different intellectual challenges built into the assignment. For all these reasons you should not expect the criteria for the gradings for a specific course to map exactly on to what we have set out here.

## 2.1 What tutors look for when marking your essays

The following is adapted from guidelines produced by the British Psychological Society (BPS, 1994) in conjunction with the Association of Heads of Psychology Departments. It is not a statement of OU policy but it should give you an idea of the sorts of *general* things tutors are likely to consider for different grade ranges. Remember that, as indicated above, what is expected for a particular OU course for a particular grade may differ from these guidelines. You should therefore always read the student notes associated with the assignment and/or ask your tutor for guidance if you are unclear what is expected. Remember, too, you don't have to do well in every area to get a particular grade. For example, your depth of insight into theoretical issues may compensate for slightly weaker coverage of the evidence, or your understanding of the material may compensate for weaknesses in the coherence of your argument. The final point to remember is that the OU's marking scheme goes up to 100 and therefore may be slightly different from ones you've been used to in the past.

## An excellent pass (85–100) is likely to:

- demonstrate comprehensive and accurate coverage of the area
- include critical evaluation
- demonstrate clarity of argument and expression
- demonstrate the ability to integrate a range of materials
- demonstrate depth of insight into theoretical issues
- demonstrate depth of understanding of the issues raised by the question
- be expressed in the author's own words
- provide full references (Level 3)

## A good pass (70–84) is likely to:

- be generally accurate and well-informed
- be reasonably comprehensive
- be well organized and structured
- address the question
- show evidence of drawing on a range of sources
- show an ability to evaluate the material, although this may be derivative
- show a good understanding of the material
- be clearly presented

## A clear pass (55–69) is likely to:

- be generally accurate, although with some omissions and errors
- give an adequate answer to the question, though with less evidence of drawing on a range of sources
- show an understanding, but probably no real development, of the arguments
- be dependent on source material
- be expressed in the author's own words
- define key terms

### A bare pass (40–54) is likely to:

- answer the question only tangentially
- miss a key point of information
- contain important inaccuracies
- show only sparse coverage of relevant material
- fail to support arguments with adequate evidence
- be over-dependent on source material

### A bare fail (30–39) is likely to:

- fail to answer the question directly
- contain very little appropriate material
- show some evidence of relevant reading but provide only cursory coverage with numerous errors, omissions or irrelevancies
- be highly disorganized
- contain much inappropriate material
- lack any real argument
- be unacceptably dependent on sources
- be plagiarized (sometimes)

### A clear fail (0–29) is likely to:

- show a profound misunderstanding of basic material
- show a complete failure to understand or answer the question
- provide totally inadequate information
- be incoherent
- be plagiarized (sometimes)

*Essays are assessed not weighed*

## 2.2 Skills you will need at different levels

As you move from Level 1 to Level 2 to Level 3 courses, the essay questions you are given should help you to develop a range of new academic skills. OU courses tend to follow a 'path'. The first essay questions that you get will recap and build on skills you have learned on lower level courses. Gradually, however, the questions will introduce you to new areas: for example, they will ask you to handle more complex theories, interrogate original texts, or use evidence in more sophisticated ways. These more advanced skills will almost certainly take you several years and a variety of courses to develop. However, on completing an OU degree you will have been introduced to a complete range of writing skills and should feel confident that you can tackle most pieces of work.

A general guide of this kind cannot give you a full breakdown of the skills that are relevant to all the different courses in the social sciences. What it tries to do is provide an outline of 'core' skills. Individual courses may emphasize different parts of these core skills or may involve specific skills of their own (for example, project writing, employing specific research methodologies, using graphs to present information). You will find help with these specific skills built into the course materials. Individual essays may also require you to emphasize some of the 'core' skills more than others. As a result of all these, you will need to adapt what we have set out here according to the demands of different questions and different courses.

We look now in detail at the 'core' skills that may be expected at the different levels. Many of these points are developed in later sections, so if you are not sure what the points 'mean', you might want to look them up.

### On completing Level I

***Introductions*** are likely to demonstrate:

- a clear understanding of the scope of the question and what is required;
- the ability to 'signpost' the shape of the essay's argument clearly and concisely;
- a basic ability to define key terms.

***The main section*** is likely to demonstrate some or all of the following, depending on what the question requires:

- an ability to construct a basic argument that engages with the question;
- the ability to précis relevant aspects of the course clearly and concisely;
- the ability to outline the basics of relevant theories;
- the ability to support arguments with appropriate evidence and examples drawn from different sources;
- an understanding that different theories are in competition, the ability to outline the main similarities and differences between these, and a basic ability to evaluate their strengths and weaknesses;
- an ability to utilize basic maps, diagrams and numerical data in a way that supports the discussion;
- some familiarity with major perspectives in the social sciences;
- some familiarity with social sciences vocabulary.

***Conclusions*** are likely to demonstrate:

- the ability to summarize the content of the essay clearly and concisely and come to a conclusion.

Quotes should be referenced, and pass essays will always need to avoid plagiarism. Essays should 'flow' smoothly, use sentences, paragraphs and grammar correctly, and be written in clear English.

## On completing Level 2

In addition to skills in all the above areas, essays show the following.

***Introductions*** are likely to demonstrate:

- a clear understanding of more complex essay questions;
- a basic ability to 'signpost' the content as well as the shape or structure of the essay but not in a laboured way;
- a grasp of the major debates that lie 'behind the question';
- an ability to define key terms.

***The main section*** is likely to demonstrate some or all of the following, depending on what the question requires:

- the ability to construct more complex arguments relevant to the question;
- the ability to 'weight' different aspects of the material according to their significance within the overall argument;
- an ability to identify and précis the key debates relevant to the question;
- the ability to outline more complex theories in a basic form;
- an ability to relate abstract ideas and theories to concrete detail;
- an ability to support arguments with appropriate evidence and examples;
- an ability to utilize information drawn from across a wide range of source materials;
- the ability to make more complex evaluations of the strengths and weaknesses of competing positions and make a reasoned choice between these;
- an ability to utilize more complex maps, diagrams and numerical data;
- a preliminary ability to work from original texts and data without relying on OU course writers' interpretations of these;
- increased familiarity with major social sciences perspectives and social sciences vocabulary and increased confidence in applying these to specific issues;
- a preliminary ability to write from 'within' specific perspectives or models;
- an ability to pull together different aspects of the course and to apply these to the essay;
- a basic ability in selecting and using appropriate quotations from, and making references to, key texts in the field.

***Conclusions*** are likely to demonstrate:

- an ability to highlight the essay's core argument;
- the ability to provide a basic summary of the key debates raised by the question and the ability to provide an overview of 'current knowledge';

- a preliminary ability to point to absences in the argument or areas worthy of future development;

Essays should also be properly referenced, be written in the author's own words, and utilize a more developed and fluent writing style (for example, by handling transitions effectively).

## On completing Level 3

In addition to skills in all of the above areas, essays may also show the following.

*Introductions* are likely to demonstrate:

- the ability to present a more sophisticated version of the essay's core argument;
- the ability to summarize in more sophisticated form the key debates raised by the question;
- the ability to provide more sophisticated definitions of terms;
- an ability to really interrogate the question by focusing on ideas or sub-questions prompted by the question in hand.

*The main section* is likely to demonstrate some or all of the following:

- the ability to construct complex arguments, 'weighting' each section according to its significance within the overall argument;
- the ability to provide sophisticated outlines of complex theories;
- the ability to support arguments with appropriate evidence and examples drawn from a wide range of sources, and to use evidence *selectively* in a way that supports central points;
- the ability to evaluate competing positions and the confidence to write from 'within' a specific perspective or model on the basis of a reasoned understanding of its strengths and weaknesses;
- familiarity with, and confidence in, handling complex maps, diagrams and numerical data;
- familiarity with, and confidence in, handling original texts and data without relying on course interpretations of these;
- familiarity with the major social sciences perspectives and social sciences vocabulary, and confidence in applying these to specific issues;

- the ability to pull together different aspects of the course and apply these to the issues raised by a specific essay question;
- the ability to use appropriate quotations and cite key texts in the field.

***Conclusions*** are likely to demonstrate:

- the ability to present a sophisticated summary of the essay's core argument;
- the ability to provide an effective synthesis of the key debates raised by the question, or a sophisticated overview of the state of 'current knowledge';
- a developed ability to point to absences in the argument or areas worthy of future development.

Essays at Level 3 should be fully referenced and written in your own words. The best essays are likely to show a significant depth of understanding of the issues raised by the question and may show a more creative or original approach (within the constraints of academic rigour).

### Different skills, same writer

In thinking about the requirements of different levels, it is important to realize that different level skills do not come neatly packaged. You may have Level 3 skills of analysis (ability to use evidence) but are still struggling with the handling of theoretical concepts and perspectives. Or you may be a whizz at your essay introductions but more shaky when it comes to putting it all together in the main section. The important point is that what we have set out are *indications* of what may be expected at different levels across the whole range of abilities, *not* that you must be able to demonstrate the appropriate level of ability in all cases. Remember too that an essay is always greater than its component parts, and it is how you put all those parts together which is often as important as the parts themselves.

## 2.3   Three golden rules for writing essays

### Rule 1: Write your answer in your own words

It's important to write in your own words because this is the best way in which you can come to understand a topic, and the only way of demonstrating this understanding to your tutor. How to avoid 'plagiarism' (or copying what someone else has already written or said) is dealt with in detail in Section 9.1. The important point to remember is that if you do plagiarize then your essay will fail. You must therefore always put arguments in your own words except when you are quoting someone directly (in which case you must provide quotation marks and the appropriate reference). The positive side of this seemingly draconian rule is that you will remember better what you have put in your own words, which is a real asset when it comes to revision.

## Rule 2: *Answer the question that is asked*

You'd be surprised how easy it is to get this wrong. At Levels 2 and 3 you will be increasingly asked to select relevant material from a range of different sources and to show why and how it is relevant. For example, you may be asked to work from units or chapters, blocks or readers, or supplementary material including cassettes and television programmes. Some courses ask you to search sources of non-OU material. On others you may be using different electronic media and computer-based information systems. The danger is in failing to select the most relevant material, or in selecting the less rather than the more relevant material, or in failing to reorganize the material in a way that best fits the question.

Make sure that you take time to read the question properly to ensure that you understand what is being asked.

## Rule 3: *Organize your material into a coherent structure*

Remember that it is unlikely that you will find the answer in just one chapter or unit, so you will need to link together a range of materials in a coherent structure of your own.

Your reader will need to understand what's going on, so be considerate – a list of unconnected ideas and examples is likely to confuse, and will certainly fail to impress. The simplest way to avoid this is to follow the kind of essay writing conventions outlined in this guide.

## 2.4 What a basic social sciences essay looks like

Okay, we know that we have to answer the question, put arguments in our own words, and organize the material into a coherent structure, but what should a social sciences essay look like?

There are different types of social sciences essay, and essays of different lengths require slightly different approaches – *these* will be addressed later in the guide. However, all social sciences essays share a basic structure. At its simplest, an essay looks something like this:

- **Title**
  Every essay should begin with the title written out in full.

- **Introduction**
  Tells the reader what the essay is about.

- **Main section**
  Develops the key points of your argument in a 'logical progression'.
  Uses evidence from research studies (empirical evidence) and theoretical arguments to support these points.

- **Conclusion**
  Reassesses the arguments in order to make a final statement in answer to the question.

- **List of references**
  Lists the publications that you've referred to in the text.

## Summary ■ ■ ■ ■ ■ ■ ■ ■ ■ ■ ■ ■ ■ ■ ■ ■ ■ ■ ■ ■ ■ ■ ■ ■ ■ ■ ■ ■

- There are three golden rules of essay writing:
  1 Write your answer in your own words.
  2 Answer the question that is asked.
  3 Organize your material into a coherent structure.
- A basic social sciences essay has the following: a title, an introduction, a main section, a conclusion, and a list of references.

■ ■ ■ ■ ■ ■ ■ ■ ■ ■ ■ ■ ■ ■ ■ ■ ■ ■ ■ ■ ■ ■ ■ ■ ■ ■ ■ ■ ■ ■ ■ ■ ■

# 3 Matching the answer to the question

Many social sciences essay questions ask you to consider one or more positions which you: advocate, or evaluate, or compare and contrast.

## 3.1 Answering advocacy questions

### Advocacy questions

Advocacy questions ask you to outline or explain and illustrate a particular issue, topic or argument. Examples of this kind of question would include:

- How have changes to the way in which the production of food is organized affected both the UK and other parts of the world? Illustrate your answer with examples.
- 'An efficient allocation of resources requires fiscal neutrality, yet the British tax system persists in encouraging some activities while discouraging others'. Explain and illustrate with examples.
- Why can the changing politics of the UK not be understood unless they are set in an international context?
- What are the basic assumptions about humanistic psychology? How are these reflected in methods for encouraging growth?

### Advocacy answers

A basic answer to an advocacy question might look something like this:

**Introduction**

**Main section**

- Provide a brief overview of the issue, topic or argument.
- Provide a more detailed breakdown of the key components of the issue, topic or argument.
- Give examples to illustrate these points.
- Briefly explore weaknesses in the viewpoint that you've been asked to advocate. Indicate alternative ways of thinking about the issues.

Or, as another example, you may decide to do the following:

- Provide a brief overview of the issue, topic or argument.
- Then, in more detail:
  outline one component of the issue, topic or argument and illustrate with an example;
  outline the second component of the issue, topic or argument and illustrate with another relevant example;
  outline the third component, … etc.
- Briefly explore weaknesses in the approach and indicate alternative ways of addressing the issues.

The exact structure of an advocacy answer will be dictated by the material and the nature of the question. When planning and drafting your essay, you should shift your argument around to identify what works best.

**Conclusion**

- Recap key points and illustrations. Give a final assessment of the usefulness of the approach.

*Remember, this is only a basic format covering the major ingredients of an advocacy question and you shouldn't follow it slavishly.*

### Advocacy questions at Levels 1, 2 and 3

By the end of Level 1 you should be able to structure an answer of this kind. As you progress through Level 2 and on to Level 3 courses you will be expected to show an increasing ability to outline and illustrate more complex positions, a greater understanding of their potential weaknesses, and an increased awareness of alternative ways of addressing the issues.

## 3.2   Answering evaluation questions

### Evaluation questions

In contrast to advocacy questions, evaluation questions ask you to explore arguments for and against a particular position or issue and to evaluate their relative strengths and weaknesses. Examples of this kind of question include:

- To what extent does citizenship depend on having a modern welfare state?

- 'Conceptual categories are clearly defined and tightly structured as hierarchically organized mental representations.' How far do you agree with this view?
- Critically evaluate the definition of work as paid employment.
- Evaluate evidence in support of theories of working memory and levels of processing. What are the implications for the modal model of memory?

## Evaluation answers

A basic evaluation answer would look something like this:

### Introduction

### Main section

- Outline the position.
- Give arguments (i.e. chains of logical reasoning) and evidence in support of the position.
- Give arguments supported by evidence which go against, question or limit the position.
- Weigh up the arguments for and against the position.

In the light of different material and different questions you may well want to adapt this basic format. For instance:

- You might start with the 'weaker' of the two arguments in the main section and follow it up with 'stronger' arguments. Will this convince the reader of your point of view more effectively?
- Rather than exploring the first position then the second and competing position, you could explore one point from position (a) and contrast it to a parallel point from position (b), then explore another point from position (a) and contrast it to another point from position (b), and so on. Does this clarify or confuse your overall argument?

As with answers to advocacy questions, you will need to decide how best to structure the arguments in the light of the question asked and the material used to answer it. Equally, you will need to emphasize different sections (the exploration of arguments for and against, the evaluation section) depending on the nature of the question.

*The trick is to adapt this basic structure to a shape that best fits your requirements.*

**Conclusion**

- Summarize, making an explicit statement as to which position (if any) you support.

## Evaluation questions at Levels 1, 2 and 3

By the end of Level 1 you should be able to structure an answer of this kind. As you progress through Level 2 and on to Level 3 courses you will be expected to show an increasing ability to compare and contrast more complex positions, greater sophistication in your analysis of their strengths and weaknesses, increased awareness of alternative ways of addressing the issues, and more confidence in showing a reasoned preference for one position over another.

# 3.3 Answering compare and contrast questions

## Compare and contrast questions

Compare and contrast questions ask you to outline points of common ground between competing positions, to explore ways in which they differ, identifying how different positions often appeal to different kinds of evidence, and, sometimes, to compare the particular positions to other positions in the same field. Examples of this kind of question include:

- Compare and contrast two different explanations of 'racial' divisions.
- Compare and contrast the views of Piaget and Mead on children's ability to take perpectives other than their own.
- In what ways do monetarist approaches differ from Keynesian approaches to the management of the UK economy? Are there any areas of agreement between them?

## Compare and contrast answers

A basic answer to a compare and contrast question might look something like this:

**Introduction**

**Main text**

- Outline position (a) and position (b).
- Identify key points of common ground between these positions and compare them.

- Identify supplementary points of common ground between these positions and compare them.
- Identify and explore key points of contrast between position (a) and position (b).
- Identify and explore supplementary points of contrast between position (a) and position (b).
- If necessary, identify and explore significant ways in which position (a) and position (b) can be contrasted to a third competing position (c).
- Briefly evaluate the merits of these positions.

Once again, you will almost certainly need to adapt this basic format to fit different questions and different material. For instance:

- There may be an obvious debate 'behind' the question that requires you to emphasize the ways in which two contrasting positions share a common orientation that is in competition with a third position. This might be the case in the third of the example questions. It read: 'In what ways do monetarist approaches differ from Keynesian approaches to the management of the UK economy? Are there any areas of agreement between them?' Here you might need to emphasize that Keynesian and monetarist approaches share a common belief in the efficacy of the capitalist market that is in strong contrast to Marxist approaches. A debate of this kind may, then, require you to scale down the extent to which you compare and contrast positions (a) and (b) in order for you to contrast them to a position (c).
- Equally, you may decide to compare a key point from positions (a) and (b) and then move straight on to contrast a key point from each position. You would then compare another point and contrast another point, and so on. This would be instead of exploring all the points of comparison in one section and then all the points of contrast in another. Ask yourself which method works best in relation to the question set and the material with which you are working.

**Conclusion**

- Summarize the major points of comparison and contrast between the positions and briefly recap which is the most persuasive and why.

### Compare and contrast questions at Levels 1, 2 and 3

By the end of Level 1 you should be able to structure a basic answer to this type of question. As you progress through Level 2 and Level 3 courses you will be expected to show an increasing ability to compare and contrast more complex positions, a greater sophistication in your analysis and a greater ability to emphasize key points, a greater confidence in showing a reasoned preference for one position over another, the ability to write from 'within' one position, and an increasing ability to relate the positions under analysis to alternative relevant positions in the same field.

## Summary ■■■■■■■■■■■■■■■■■■■■■■■■■■■■■■■■■■

- Advocacy questions ask you to outline and illustrate a particular issue, topic or argument.

- Evaluation questions ask you to explore arguments for and against competing positions and to evaluate their relative strengths and weaknesses.

- Compare and contrast questions ask you to identify and explore points of comparison and contrast between competing positions.

- These basic structures should be adapted in the light of the question and the material under discussion.

- As you progress from Level 1 through to Levels 2 and 3 courses you will be expected to show greater confidence in handling complex material and increasingly sophisticated powers of analysis.

■■■■■■■■■■■■■■■■■■■■■■■■■■■■■■■■■■■■■■■■

# 4 Be prepared

Thorough preparation and planning is the basis of any good piece of written work, and it really is worth putting some effort into it. Here are some reminders for those of you already experienced in essay planning, and some suggestions for anyone coming to OU social sciences essay writing for the first time. (Bear in mind also the three golden rules for essay writing in Section 2.3 above.)

## 4.1 Look back

If this is not your first essay, and if you haven't done so already, take a look at your previous one. Did your tutor make any suggestions that you need to bear in mind for this essay? Did you learn anything else about essay writing? Note down these points. (A checklist of activities for what to do when your essay is returned to you is given in Appendix A.)

## 4.2 Read the question

- Identify the process or 'command' words (for example, 'discuss', 'evaluate', 'explore'). These tell you *how* you have to answer the question. A list of these words and relevant definitions for each are in Appendix B.
- Identify the 'content' words. These tell you *what* you have to write about.

Let's consider the question:

'The family in Britain is in crisis'. Discuss.

'Discuss' is the command word (implying that you have to explore the evidence for and against the statement), and 'family', 'Britain', and 'crisis' are the content words. So, the evidence that you need to explore should focus on whether there is a crisis in the family in Britain and what 'crisis' might mean in this context.

## 4.3 Identify the relevant material

- Read the guidance notes that you get with each question. These will prevent a lot of unnecessary suffering and should always be consulted.

- Read through any existing notes that you have, read or re-read all necessary parts of the course (or non-course material where you are told to do this), and note all relevant material.

## 4.4  Organize the material

- 'Brainstorm' your ideas for the essay on paper (that is, jot down a list of questions and issues prompted by the question, all the relevant examples you can think of, and any other related evidence); recheck notes and add left-out material; then link connected ideas and points. (Appendix C has an example of one way of doing this called a 'mind map'.)
- Collate and write out these points on separate sheets of paper, on 'post-its', or on index cards.
- Shuffle these until you've got them in a logical order (Section 6 below offers ideas for creating a 'logical progression' in your argument). This is your essay plan.
- Ideas may come to you at unexpected moments – for these keep a notebook handy and jot them down.

If you have a word processor, you may want to do some of this on your screen. (See also Appendix F for details.)

## 4.5  First draft to final version

- Working from your essay plan, begin writing a first draft. You may need to revise your plan as the essay takes shape. Don't worry, this is perfectly normal!
- It may help to write out the question at the beginning of your first draft so that you keep its exact wording in front of you to ensure you are answering the question that is asked.
- Do the best you can but see it as a first draft and expect to make some improvements – you may even want to prepare a second draft – before writing the final version.
- We all know that people sometimes put their first draft straight in the post. If you have time, always put the essay aside for at least a day to let the dust settle, show it to a friend or another student to get feedback, and then reread the question and the essay yourself. Its strengths and weaknesses should now be a lot clearer to you.

- You're now in a position to write your definitive answer. Now is the time to consider more carefully your presentation (sentence structure, grammar, etc.) and to check for clarity of expression.
- When this is complete, fill in your PT3 (the OU's essay cover-sheet), put the whole lot in the post, and await your tutor's comments with quiet confidence.

The next sections of this guide offer more detailed help through the process of first attempt to final version – in short, writing your essay! One experience of producing a social sciences essay, on a word processor, is given in Appendix F where you can see how from the earliest brainstorming stage a good essay emerged.

## Summary ■ ■ ■ ■ ■ ■ ■ ■ ■ ■ ■ ■ ■ ■ ■ ■ ■ ■ ■ ■ ■ ■ ■ ■ ■ ■ ■ ■ ■ ■

- Essay planning has six principal stages:
  > reading and understanding the question;
  > identifying the relevant material;
  > making an essay plan;
  > writing a first draft;
  > reviewing the first draft, maybe writing a second draft;
  > writing a final version.
- The complete process of preparing an essay on a word processor is described in Appendix F.

■ ■ ■ ■ ■ ■ ■ ■ ■ ■ ■ ■ ■ ■ ■ ■ ■ ■ ■ ■ ■ ■ ■ ■ ■ ■ ■ ■ ■ ■ ■ ■ ■ ■ ■ ■ ■ ■

# 5 Writing introductions

There is more than one way to write an introduction, so your own work doesn't have to follow slavishly the advice given here. However, one common way to write an introduction is to treat it like an 'abstract', that is, a brief synopsis of the central points raised in the essay. This is the approach we'll explore in this section. In addition, it's worth remembering that shorter essays (1,000–1,500 words) will probably require something punchy and concise, while longer essays (1,500 words and over) can afford an introduction that covers more ground. Like other areas of essay writing, you will probably find that you get better at introductions the more experienced you become. It is certainly fair to say that Level 3 courses will expect more from your introductions than courses at Levels 1 and 2. By the end of Level 1 you should be able to identify the subject of the essay and begin to highlight its key themes or arguments. By the end of a Level 3 course you should aim to display a firm grasp of the central debates that lie 'behind' the question and provide a sophisticated version of your own core arguments. Some tutors, particularly at Level 3, will also want you to 'establish a position' in the introduction. This section explores all these issues by looking in depth at:

- longer or 'full' introductions for essays over 1,500 words long;
- basic short introductions for essays 1,000 to 1,500 words long.

## 5.1 Longer or 'full' introductions

Full introductions can be written as a section in their own right and, in certain circumstances, may well be several paragraphs long. As a rough guide, a full introduction should be 5 to 10 per cent of your total word count.

'Full' introductions generally do most of the following: identify the subject of the essay; signpost the shape of the argument; highlight the major debates that lie 'behind' the question; signpost the content of the argument; define terms; (sometimes) establish a position. We consider each of these features in more detail below.

### Identifying the subject of the essay

The easiest way to do this is to refer back to the question. For example, if the essay question states, 'Evaluate the claim that

*Coronation Street* is the most enjoyable contemporary British soap opera', you might want to write:

> This essay will evaluate the claim that *Coronation Street* is the most enjoyable contemporary British soap opera.

However, you can always be more creative than this. For example, you might write:

> *Coronation Street* consistently received higher ratings than any other British soap opera. This essay explores the basis of this popularity, evaluating its appeal in comparison to two other major contemporary British soap operas: *Eastenders* and *Brookside*.

## Signposting the shape of the argument

The intention here is to give the reader a 'road map' of the essay. At its simplest this involves highlighting the main stages of your argument. For instance, you might write:

> The first section focuses on … This argument is developed in the following section which explores …

Identifying the shape of your argument in this manner is called 'signposting'.

## Highlighting major debates and signposting the content of the argument

Essay questions will often revolve round a key debate or debates: for example, 'Does the First World exploit the Third World?' or 'Is behaviour biologically or socially produced?'. Often these debates will not be referred to explicitly but will lie 'behind' or be implied in the question asked. Your introduction will need to pull out these debates and signpost your essay's responses to them. This will form the core of your argument. Referring back to the soap opera example on the popularity of *Coronation Street* and the difference in style between it and the 'gritty realism' of *Eastenders* and *Brookside*: the question is whether *Coronation Street*'s less naturalistic style is more appealing to audiences or whether people are more drawn in by the focus on big social issues in *Eastenders* and *Brookside*? This might well be one of the crucial debates that lies 'behind' the question 'Evaluate the claim that *Coronation Street* is the most enjoyable contemporary British soap opera'. Your introduction could therefore refer to this debate. It might look like this:

*Coronation Street* consistently receives higher ratings than any other British soap opera. This essay explores the basis of this popularity, evaluating its appeal in comparison to two other major contemporary British soap operas: *Eastenders* and *Brookside*. In the process, the essay will analyse *Coronation Street*'s use of strong female characters, its exploration of women's lives, and its humorous treatment of male characters. It will contrast these to the 'gritty realism' favoured by *Eastenders* and *Brookside*.

However, you will see that this introduction not only discusses *Coronation Street*'s style in opposition to the 'gritty realism' of *Eastenders* and *Brookside*, but also suggests that its appeal lies in its strong women characters and humorous treatment of men. In doing this it signposts the content of the essay's argument: *Coronation Street*'s less naturalistic style revolves round strong women characters and humorous treatment of men, and that this is a core reason that underpins its popularity.

## Defining terms

People can often be over-enthusiastic about defining terms. You don't need to define absolutely everything, particularly terms that are in widespread everyday use. Nevertheless, definitions can be useful in relation to the following:

- *Key concepts and obviously technical terms*
  For example, if you are asked to assess critically a particular theory or concept (say, the notion of familial ideology, or core–periphery models of development, or cognitive developmental theory) it is fairly obvious that you will need to provide a definition or outline of it. In fact, you may decide that it is more appropriate to define such a theory or concept (perhaps in a section of its own immediately after the introduction) simply because it will require several sentences and will look over-long and clumsy if included with your other introductory remarks.

- *Terms that are contested*
  For instance, the question:

  > Is the family in Britain in crisis?

  hinges on how you define 'crisis'. For some people rising post-war divorce rates and the increasing profile of feminism and lesbian and gay rights constitute a 'crisis'. Other people find these developments positive or less problematic. Here you would need to point to the contested nature of the term and highlight the fact that it is open to competing definitions.

- *Theories or approaches that have different versions*
  Particularly at Level 3, where there is a greater emphasis on theoretical sophistication, you will need to define the particular version of the theory or approach that you are using. For example, it may not be enough to say that you will use a 'Marxist analysis' because there are competing versions of Marxist theory.

### Establishing a position

Establishing a position means indicating the particular 'line' that you intend to take in an essay. For example, our *Coronation Street* introduction could be adapted to read:

> *Coronation Street* consistently receives higher ratings than any other British soap opera. This essay explores the basis of this popularity, evaluating its appeal in comparison to two other major contemporary British soap operas: *Eastenders* and *Brookside*. In its opening section, the essay uses feminist ideas, analysing *Coronation Street's* appeal in terms of its 'women-centredness': in particular, its focus on strong female characters, its exploration of women's lives, and its often humorous treatment of men. The essay then goes on to contrast this approach to the more naturalistic 'gritty realism' of *Eastenders* and *Brookside* which focus on social issues like unemployment and HIV but which fail to address women's lives as successfully as does *Coronation Street*. As a result, the essay argues that the non-naturalistic but strongly women-centred aspects of *Coronation Street* are central to its appeal, particularly to a female audience.

Here we have indicated that the essay is based on a feminist reading of soap operas.

## 5.2 Basic short introductions

In a very short essay you may only have between 50 and 100 words to tell your reader what the essay is about. As a result, your introduction will need to be concise and highly focused. It should still:

- identify the subject of the essay and define key terms;
- highlight any major debates that lie 'behind' the question;
- signpost the essay's key argument.

'I cut out only necessary words'

However, it would probably stop there. Thus a short introduction to the same question 'Evaluate the claim that *Coronation Street* is the most enjoyable contemporary British soap opera' might now read:

> *Coronation Street* consistently receives higher ratings than any other British soap opera. This essay explores the basis of this popularity, evaluating its appeal in comparison to two other major contemporary British soap operas: *Eastenders* and *Brookside*. In the process, the essay will analyse *Coronation Street*'s use of strong female characters, its exploration of women's lives, and its humorous treatment of male characters. It will contrast these to the 'gritty realism' favoured by *Eastenders* and *Brookside*.

Outlining the content of your core argument will alert your reader to what is most important about the essay, or what makes it 'hang together'.

## 5.3 When do you write the introduction?

The difficulty with introduction writing is that sometimes you only know what the core arguments are when you have finished your essay. So although writing the introduction can help to give you a clear idea of what you are doing, you may find that it is a good idea to write it last, though you will often find that you can also write a good introduction at second draft stage. If you then want to revise the introduction at the end of the second draft, you may want to get out some scissors, cut off your existing version and Sellotape the better one to your page. If you have access to a word processor you can, of course, do this on screen.

## Summary ■■■■■■■■■■■■■■■■■■■■■■■■■■■■■■■

- Introductions tell the reader what your essay is about. You may write it first to give you an idea of what you are doing, or you may find that you can write a better introduction when you have completed the main bulk of your essay.

- There is more than one way to write an introduction. The approach adopted here treats the introduction as an 'abstract' or synopsis of key points.

- 'Full' introductions: identify the subject of the essay; signpost the shape of the argument; highlight the major debates that lie 'behind' the question; signpost the content of the argument; (where necessary) define terms; (sometimes) establish a position or look ahead to the conclusion.

- A basic short introduction should tell the reader what the essay is about by: identifying the subject of the essay; highlighting the major debates that lie 'behind' the question; identifying the essay's key argument(s) or theme(s).

- By the end of Level 1 your introductions should be proficient at identifying the subject of the essay, and signposting the shape of the argument.

- At Level 2, introductions should move towards hightlighting the major debates raised by the essay question, signposting the content of the argument, defining terms effectively, and (if appropriate) establishing a position.

- Level 3 introductions should show greater sophistication in bringing out the major debates raised by the question, signposting the content of the argument, defining terms, and (if appropriate) establishing a position.

- Full introductions should normally be between 5 and 10 per cent of the total; short introductions may need to be 50–100 words.

■■■■■■■■■■■■■■■■■■■■■■■■■■■■■■■■■■■■■

# 6 Writing the main section

Before you begin drafting your main section you may find it helpful to look back at Section 3, 'Matching the answer to the question', particularly the guidance on how to make your main section address appropriately the type of question you are answering.

## 6.1 Structuring your argument

Essays need a strong and coherent structure if you are to convince your reader of your case. Central to this is the process of building an argument, that is, making each point follow on from the previous one. The guidance notes for one OU course (The Open University, 1994) suggests that creating a logical progression to a social sciences argument is not dissimilar to the way we argue in everyday life. The author imagines what may be said in a discussion about whether it is better to shop at Waitrose rather than Sainsbury. This is his answer (which he stresses is not intended to bear any relation to the facts).

'I think you'd be better off shopping at Waitrose.'

'It's a lot more convenient than Sainsbury's and they have a wider range of goods and the stuff's better quality. Their staff always seem to know the store inside out and can tell you whether or not they stock a particular item and what shelf it's on. And they're a lot friendlier there.'

'Waitrose is convenient because there are seldom long queues to wait in. That means you don't have to spend more time waiting to pay for your stuff than it took you to go around the store gathering it in.'

'My girlfriend likes chocolates, and Waitrose stock chocolates you've probably never heard of before. My girlfriend's always amazed at what I bring home.' Etc. Etc. …

(The Open University, 1994, p.35)

The author argues that if we look at this imagined reply carefully we can see a logical progression to it: that is, we can see the way it builds an argument. If we break it down it looks something like this:

- *Outlines a particular point of view*
  'I think you'd be better off shopping at Waitrose.'

- *Gives reasons for holding this view*
  'It's a lot more convenient than Sainsbury's ... they have a wider range of goods ... the stuff's better quality', and so on.
- *Gives evidence (in an essay he might also cite theoretical arguments) to back up these claims*
  Waitrose is convenient because 'there are seldom long queues to wait in'; they have a wider range of goods because they 'stock chocolates you've probably never heard of'.

If you're the sort of person who likes diagrams you can represent the stages of this process in a similar way to those in Figure 1.

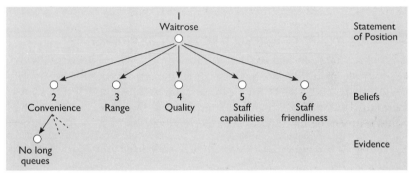

*Figure 1*
*'Waitrose vs Sainsbury' essay: logical progression to argue Waitrose is best*
Source: The Open University, 1994, p.37

Of course, if this had been a formal essay, the writer would have had to complete it with some kind of evaluation (a section pointing to the limitations as well as the strengths of their argument) together with a summary of the main points.

## Summary ■■■■■■■■■■■■■■■■■■■■■■■■■■■■■■■■

- The argument in the main section of an essay needs to have 'logical progression'.
- We construct logically progressing arguments in everyday life.
- Logical progression involves: outlining a particular point of view; giving reasons why this point of view might be correct; and providing evidence to support these claims.

■■■■■■■■■■■■■■■■■■■■■■■■■■■■■■■■■■■■■■■■

## 6.2 Supporting your argument (using evidence)

Increasingly at Levels 2 and 3, you will be asked to construct an argument from a range of different sources. For example, in the OU you might need to bring together different kinds of material from different course units, from reader chapters, supplementary articles, reports, maps, statistical data, television and radio programmes or course cassettes, other electronic media, and in some cases non-OU material, including where appropriate your own experience. You will then need to reorganize this material in a way that answers the question. You will also need to select from the range of sources the appropriate evidence which supports your argument.

### Selecting evidence – using a range of examples

Any essay question will expect you to support your arguments with appropriate examples and evidence. However, as you progress from Level 1 to Level 2 and Level 3 courses you will be expected to show increased skill at selecting the examples that illustrate and support your points most effectively. As a general rule:

- *Highlight examples that have the most significant or far-reaching implications.*
  The examples will need to be relevant to the question and engage with the point that you are making. This means being selective. You cannot cite every single related example or piece of evidence in the course. Some of them will be more useful to your purpose than others, and you will need to identify these and relate them to the issue under discussion.

- *Where possible, support your argument with more than one example.*
  Unless the point is a minor one, single examples should be avoided (unless you are clearly directed to use them) since they are unlikely to cover the range of issues that you will need to highlight.

- *Select examples from a range of sources.*
  Particularly at Levels 2 and 3, you will need to look for relevant examples from across the course. As suggested above, in the OU you might need to draw material from many different course components and sometimes from non-OU material as well. In looking for other material you may also want to look for more topical illustrations, especially when a course has been available for some time.

- *Work from the general to the particular.*
  Specific examples should be used to support general arguments. Whereas a general argument cannot necessarily be induced from only one or two concrete examples, one or two concrete examples can be used to illustrate the truth of a general argument on the grounds that there are many more examples of the same point but it is not possible to cite them in your essay.

### Selecting evidence – using empirical evidence

Social scientists carry out research studies to gather evidence to back up their theories and arguments. Evidence from such research is called empirical evidence (meaning information collected through our senses), and since it comes from systematic, checkable investigation it is more highly regarded than everyday examples or personal experience. Course materials contain many examples of research studies, and a good essay will use empirical evidence to support the arguments made. This involves not simply describing a piece of research carried out into the topic you are discussing but to make clear how the results of the research supports or illustrates your arguments. For example:

> The experiences of being in a group will affect how other groups are seen. (argument)

> This has been demonstrated by Sherif et al. (1956) when groups of American summer camp students were formed into various competing groups.
> (research study described)

> The experience of being in a group affected behaviour, making them antagonistic towards those in other groups.
> (results of study described, showing clear link with argument)

Information from research studies is one particular type of evi-dence which you might wish to use in your essay. However, the general rules on selecting evidence given above also apply to other sources of empirical evidence.

### Selecting evidence – using maps, diagrams, numerical data

Maps, diagrams or numerical data are further major sources of evidence that you can use to illustrate and support your argument. Although the use of numerical data may not always be explicitly called for, you will always gain extra marks for judicial use of such data where relevant. Maps, diagrams and numerical data, rather like quotations, should be used to illustrate and support points in your argument and not to replace it, so always remember to integrate them into the points you are making.

If you reproduce maps, diagrams or numerical data you will need to give your sources for them. However, it is often sufficient to refer to them, for example, by saying 'As the data used by Smith shows (Smith, 1995, p.15, Table 1) ...', and providing a full reference at the end of your essay (references are dealt with in detail in Section 8 and Appendix D). In addition, remember that maps, tables and graphs are not hard facts. You will need to be critical of your sources by, for example, bearing in mind what scale is being used and how this shapes the evidence, by questioning how data has been collected, or by asking how a graph would change if plotted over a wider time-scale. You should also be aware that numerical data represent specific outcomes and that the underlying causes of those outcomes will be unclear and will need further investigation. For example, it is quite possible for different combinations of causes to produce a similar numerical outcome.

## Using theory, being 'critical'

Essay questions will often require you to explore theoretical arguments as well as concrete examples, and you will also want to draw on other people's theories as evidence to support your own argument. By the end of Level 1 you will need to be able to demonstrate an understanding of competing theoretical positions in your essay writing and be able to identify the fundamental strengths and weaknesses of each. Level 2 and 3 courses build on these skills, and will increasingly expect you to read original articles or extracts (rather than relying on course authors' explanations of someone else's theory), demonstrate an understanding of more complex theoretical positions, and be more confident in expressing a reasoned preference for one theoretical position over another.

In working with theories remember that they are like spectacles: we put on one pair and we see the world in a Marxist way; we put on another pair and we see the world in a feminist way. As a result, we have to accept that theories do not let us see the world 'as it is'; we see only what they allow us to see. In fact, many social scientists argue that you can never see the world 'as it is' and that you always have to look at it from one perspective or another. The task is to find a pair of spectacles that allow us to view the object under study in as useful a way as possible. These points have some important implications:

- Competing theories are not all equal. Different theories appeal to different kinds of evidence. Different theories are 'useful' in different contexts.

- You cannot lump together the good bits of a whole range of theories to make one 'super theory'. Different theories will contradict each other. As a result, incorporating an insight from one theory into an existing approach will often require a radical restructuring of *both*.

- Even when you can make a new theory from aspects of previous ones, you still won't have a view of the world 'as it really is'. You may have a more powerful pair of spectacles to look through but you will still have to ask yourself the following questions: Is there something beyond the range of these spectacles that I can't see? Are these spectacles still obscuring what I can see? If I turn to look at a new object, do my spectacles work as well as they did when I looked at the first object? Asking these sorts of questions is called being 'critical'. This doesn't mean being negative about everything. It means 'standing outside' a theory, looking for its limitations as well as its strengths.

## Being 'self-reflective'

This means being aware of your own prejudices and letting the reader know about them. This is important because at some point choosing between competing arguments always involves making a value judgement. While it may be possible to identify clear reasons why some arguments are more persuasive than others, your choice will almost inevitably be coloured by your political, moral and philosophical values. It is therefore important to make explicit the theoretical/political orientation that underpins your essay rather than pretending that your argument is simply 'objective'. For example, you might indicate that the essay is being written from 'within' a feminist, Marxist, or cognitive development theory perspective. This will alert the reader to possible bias or areas of partiality in your argument and will allow them to make up their own mind about the strengths of your case. In fact, by signalling your possible blind spots to the reader, you are being more objective than if you pretended such blind spots didn't exist.

## *Summary* ■ ■ ■ ■ ■ ■ ■ ■ ■ ■ ■ ■ ■ ■ ■ ■ ■ ■ ■ ■ ■ ■ ■ ■ ■ ■ ■ ■ ■

- As you progress from Level 1 and through Level 2 and Level 3 courses you will increasingly be required to select relevant material from a range of sources and relate this back to the individual essay question.

- Arguments should be supported with appropriate illustrations and evidence. Try to select a range of the most significant examples: some are richer and more far-reaching than others. Examples should relate back to the essay question and engage with the argument that you are making.

- For some courses you will need to use maps, diagrams or numerical data. These should be used as evidence to support your argument, but remember, they are not 'hard facts'.

- Social sciences essays often ask you to explore theoretical arguments and use these as evidence as well as concrete examples. As you develop your essay writing skills you will need to show increasing confidence in exploring the strengths and weaknesses of competing theories.

- Some theories are stronger and more convincing than others; theories can't necessarily be lumped together to make a 'super theory' – they often contradict each other. In handling theories social scientists need to be 'critical', that is, they need to display an awareness of a theory's weaknesses and its strengths.

- Being 'self-reflective' means acknowledging your own particular biases, for example, by indicating that you are arguing from a specific point of view.

■ ■ ■ ■ ■ ■ ■ ■ ■ ■ ■ ■ ■ ■ ■ ■ ■ ■ ■ ■ ■ ■ ■ ■ ■ ■ ■ ■ ■ ■ ■ ■ ■ ■ ■

## 6.3 Adding weight to your argument

Social scientists highlight key works and use quotations for the following reasons:

- as a source of evidence, that is, to support and illustrate their own points;

- to provide the reader with a 'map' of the most important work done in the area under discussion;

- to demonstrate to the reader that they have thought about and understood what other people have written on a subject and that their own arguments should be taken seriously.

From the end of Level 1 you will be increasingly expected to be able to select appropriate quotations and cite key texts to add weight to your argument.

Let's take a brief look at some of these strategies in operation. Here is an example of one writer, the film theorist Richard Dyer, highlighting key texts to support an argument of his own. First he sets up his point, arguing that the way men are able to look at women reproduces gender relations of power. He writes:

> 'One of the things I really envy about men,' a friend once said to me, 'is the right to look.' She went on to point out how in public places, on the street, at meetings, men could look freely at women, but that women could only look back surreptitiously, against the grain of their upbringing … [This is] so utterly routine … that we probably don't remark on it, yet it encapsulates, and effectively reinforces, one of the fundamental ways by which power relations between the sexes are maintained.

> (Dyer, 1989, p.198)

Having stated his own point, Dyer goes on to cite existing research to back up his claims. He argues:

> In her book *Body Politics*[1] Nancy M. Henley examines the very many different non-verbal ways that gender roles and male power are constantly being rebuilt and reaffirmed. She does for gesture, body posture, facial expressions and so on what, most recently, Dale Spender's *Man Made Language*[2] does for verbal communication, and shows how non-verbal communication is both a register of male–female relations and one of the means by which those relations are kept the way they are.

> (Dyer, 1989, pp.198–9)

In this passage, Richard Dyer uses Nancy M. Henley's and Dale Spender's work as evidence to support his own argument. The fact that these writers have already argued a similar case to Dyer's lends his claim weight and authority, and tells the reader that he has done his background reading and knows what he's talking about.

The feminist psychologist, Janet Sayers, deploys a similar strategy in the following extract. This time, however, she uses a quotation to back up her point.

> Feminism involves keeping in clear focus at one and the same time the fact that as individuals women share the same aspirations as

men, and the fact that as women they are systematically obstructed by our society from realizing these aspirations. The radical feminist, Andrea Dworkin, points this out when she says:

> The liberation of women requires facing the real condition of women in order to change it. 'We're all just people' is a stance that prohibits recognition of the systematic cruelties visited on women because of sex oppression.
> (Dworkin, 1983: 217)

(Sayers, 1986, p.173)

There are several things that are worth pulling out of these examples:

- In each case, the writers use their quotation or reference to another author to support a point that they themselves have already made. This is important because there is a temptation to let quotations in particular do the work for you. Quotations and references to other people's work should support rather than replace your argument.
- Both writers are very careful to provide *references* for the works that they cite. We look at references in more detail later in Section 8.
- Sayers is very careful to *introduce* her quotation with the phrase, 'The radical feminist, Andrea Dworkin, points this out when she says …'. Quotations that aren't introduced in some way read as if they have appeared out of nowhere and interrupt the 'flow' of the writing.
- Sayers has indented her quotation from Andrea Dworkin. All quotations need to be identified. It's usual to indent longer quotations to distinguish them from your own argument. Shorter quotations don't need to be indented, but need to be enclosed in single inverted commas.
- Shortening or adding to your quoted material needs to be shown. If you leave out irrelevant phrases, indicate such cuts with three dots (…) known as an ellipsis. Similarly, if you need to add or substitute a word or phrase to clarify the sense, put your inserted words in square brackets; for example: 'They were important because …' becomes '[Peggy and Jack] were important because …'.

## Summary ■ ■ ■ ■ ■ ■ ■ ■ ■ ■ ■ ■ ■ ■ ■ ■ ■ ■ ■ ■ ■ ■ ■ ■ ■ ■ ■ ■ ■

- Quotations and references to key texts are used: as a source of evidence; to provide the reader with a 'map' of the most important works in an area; and to give the work 'authority'.

- Quotations should be introduced.

- Longer quotations should be written in a separate paragraph indented at the left-hand margin. Shorter quotations can be written in the main text in single inverted commas. Any changes should be indicated.

- Quotations and key texts highlighted in an essay should be supported by a reference.

- By Level 2 you will increasingly be expected to be able to select appropriate quotations and cite key texts in support of your argument.

■ ■ ■ ■ ■ ■ ■ ■ ■ ■ ■ ■ ■ ■ ■ ■ ■ ■ ■ ■ ■ ■ ■ ■ ■ ■ ■ ■ ■ ■ ■ ■

## 6.4 Communicating your argument to the reader

You may feel happy that you have grasped the essay question and are able to answer it comprehensively and logically, but to prove this you will need to be able to convey your ideas, to communicate them to your reader.

*Well ... er ... this is it.*

## Thinking about the audience

Students often ask who their reader is meant to be. Perhaps the best way to think about this at Levels 1 and 2 is to assume that your reader is someone studying social sciences at the same level as you but at another university. You can assume that your reader will have a grasp of basic social sciences ideas, so you won't need to explain every last detail to them. However, they won't necessarily be studying the same things as you are, so you will need to explain more complex ideas and be careful to define your terms. At Level 3 you can assume that your reader will have a greater degree of sophistication and you can therefore afford to write with more complexity. In fact, by the end of a Level 3 course you should aim to be writing for an expert audience.

## Clear sentences and paragraphs

The general rule in essay writing is to keep your sentences simple and easily understood. However, like other academic fields, the social sciences tend to have formal written styles and specialized vocabularies. Social sciences vocabulary can't be dismissed simply as 'jargon' (although sometimes this might be a justified criticism). Academic disciplines need a complex language to be able to deal with complex issues. Unfortunately, this may cause you problems. There is a real danger that in trying to sound 'academic' you may simply sound confused. Our advice is, if you're unsure, keep things simple. Even when you feel more confident you need to remember that there is nothing to be gained from using complex language for its own sake. The real test lies in being able to communicate complex ideas in the form that is most easily understood.

Equally, your paragraphs need to be as clear and straightforward as possible. The 'Rubin method' of paragraph analysis (Rubin, 1983) suggests that paragraphs have

- a topic;
- a series of statements that explain what the author thinks is special or relevant about the topic;

and that, put together, these form the paragraph's

- main idea.

Thus each paragraph should address one key point or one aspect of a key point. A 1,500 word essay is likely to have five or six key points as well as an introduction and conclusion.

## Giving the essay direction

If the reader is to avoid getting lost in your argument you need to tell them what is happening at key points along the way. There are three effective ways to do this:

- introduce and summarize the main sections;
- recap and signpost your argument;
- where useful, refer back to the question.

### Introducing and summarizing main sections

To illustrate this point, here is an example from a reading by Alan Walker. Walker is exploring the development of 'community care' policy in the 1980s and early 1990s. He has just discussed the growth of private old people's homes and is now going on to look at the policy of closing long-stay institutions for people with poor mental health.

This is how he handles the transition:

> So far this discussion has concentrated on private care from the perspective of service users, partly in order to dispel the myth of choice that is usually associated with the private sector. But, while the quality of care is substandard in some private homes, there is also plenty of evidence to show that the pay and conditions of staff working in some of them is well below their public counterparts. There are documented examples too of untrained and low-paid staff having to bear high levels of responsibility for the care of vulnerable people and being threatened with dismissal if they join a trade union (Holmes and Johnson, 1988, p.xix).
>
> At the same time as imposing severe resource constraints on local authorities and encouraging the rapid growth of private residential and nursing homes, the government embarked on a radical programme of mental health hospital closure. The policy of hospital run-down, particularly of mental illness facilities, dates back to the Hospital Plan of 1962.
>
> (Walker, 1994, p.33)

If we break down this passage we can see Walker doing the following:

- He first reiterates the key point from his previous discussion (despite market rhetoric, the growth in private residential care has not resulted in increased choice for old people), thus underscoring and concluding the argument of this section.

- He next creates a bridge between this first section and his new point ('At the same time as imposing severe resource constraints on local authorities and encouraging the rapid growth of private residential and nursing homes').
- Finally, he introduces the theme of his new section (the 'programme of mental health hospital closure').

## Recapping and signposting

Throughout his article Walker recaps and signposts his argument. For instance, he writes:

> Together these policy developments, taken with those reviewed earlier, suggest a strategy aimed at residualizing the social services. The issue of how far the Griffiths Report and the White Paper chime with this strategy will be discussed in the next section. For the moment the three main dimensions to the policy may be summarized.
>
> In the first place, ...
>
> (Walker, 1994, p.35)

Particularly in longer pieces of work, recapping and signposting provides the reader with a strong sense of the argument's direction.

## Referring back to the question

This is the final strategy you can use to stop your reader getting lost in the argument. However, it is important not to be too laborious about this. For example, constantly repeating the essay title in full can sometimes sound clumsy. You don't necessarily want your essay peppered with phrases like 'In answering the question "Evaluate the importance of the unconscious in Freud's model of the mind" it is thus necessary to ...'. You can often reference the question more simply by picking out and reusing a key phrase. For instance, the title of Walker's paper is 'Community care policy: from consensus to conflict', and throughout his article Walker reminds the reader that 'community care policy' is the subject of discussion. For instance, he writes 'The post-war political consensus on community care policy was sustained by...', 'While the primary intention of community care policy during the 1980s and early 1990s appears to have been ...' (Walker, 1994, pp.30, 31). Phrases like this will pull the reader's attention back to the subject of your essay.

## Making your essay 'flow'

Link words and sentences are used to make an essay 'flow', that is, they make the writing easy to read. Let's take another look at Walker's article (p.47). If we took out all the link words and phrases, the extract would read something like this:

> The notion of choice usually associated with the private sector is a myth. There is evidence to show that the pay and conditions of staff working in some private homes is well below that of their public counterparts. There are documented examples of untrained and low-paid staff having to bear high levels of responsibility for the care of vulnerable people and being threatened with dismissal if they join a trade union (Holmes and Johnson, 1988, p.xix).
>
> The government has embarked on a radical programme of mental health hospital closure.

Without the link words and phrases, the extract reads like a list of points or something written in note form, and the reader is jolted from one issue to another. In making sure that you link sentences and paragraphs, you thus ensure that your reader's attention sticks to the argument and doesn't get distracted by your writing.

## Summary ■■■■■■■■■■■■■■■■■■■■■■■■■■■■■■■■

- At Levels 1 and 2 your notional reader is someone studying social sciences at an equivalent level in another University. They will understand basic social sciences concepts but won't necessarily be familiar with the area addressed in your essay. By the end of a Level 3 course you should aim to write for an 'expert' audience.

- The point of essay writing is to convey complex ideas in as clear a form as possible.

- Paragraphs contain a topic and a series of statements explaining what is relevant about this topic. Together these make up its 'main idea'. A 1,500 word essay will have five or six key points plus an introduction and conclusion.

- You can give your essay a strong sense of direction by: introducing and summarizing main sections; recapping and signposting your argument; where useful, referring back to the question.

- Using link words and sentences ensures that your essay 'flows' smoothly.

■■■■■■■■■■■■■■■■■■■■■■■■■■■■■■■■■■■■■■■■

# 7 Writing conclusions

Conclusions are an important part of an essay, and a well written conclusion is a good way of picking up extra marks. The primary job of a conclusion is to provide a final condensed version of the essay's core argument and in the process to provide an overview of the state of 'current knowledge' or 'current opinion' on any one topic. Since your conclusion should take up no more than 10 per cent of your essay, a short essay (1,000 to 1,500 words long) won't have room to do much more than this. However, if you're writing a longer essay (1,500 words and over) your conclusion should do the following:

- recap the key points in your argument/summarize the key debates raised by the question; and try to synthesize them;
- provide a final condensed version of the essay's core argument that restates your position on the question;
- if necessary, identify absences in your argument that could be explored in future work.

Put simply, a conclusion should leave the reader with a clear impression of your argument: what it was about, what you believe, and why you believe this. By the end of a Level 1 course your conclusions should demonstrate the ability to summarize the content of the essay clearly and concisely. At Levels 2 and 3 you will be expected to progress towards writing more complex conclusions that emphasize condensed versions of your core argument. How do you do this?

If you have read the section on writing introductions, you will remember the following question and introduction:

Evaluate the claim that *Coronation Street* is the most enjoyable contemporary British Soap opera.

*Coronation Street* consistently receives higher ratings than any other British soap opera. This essay explores the basis of this popularity, evaluating its appeal in comparison to two other major contemporary British soap operas: *Eastenders* and *Brookside*. In its opening section, the essay uses feminist ideas, analysing *Coronation Street*'s appeal in terms of its 'women-centredness': in particular, its focus on strong female characters, its exploration of women's lives, and its often humorous treatment of men. The essay then goes on to contrast this approach to the more naturalistic 'gritty realism' of *Eastenders* and *Brookside* which focus on social issues like unemployment and HIV but which, arguably, fail to address women's lives as successfully as does *Coronation Street*. As a result, the essay argues that the non-naturalistic but strongly women-centred aspects of *Coronation Street* are central to its appeal, particularly with a female audience.

Imagine that we now have to write a conclusion to the same essay. We will have written a main section that develops these arguments and provides detailed supporting evidence to back up and illustrate our claims. We now have to bring the essay to a close, leaving the reader with a clear overall impression of our argument and our reasons for holding this position. From the introduction it's clear that the main thrust of our argument is that *Coronation Street*'s appeal lies in the way it speaks to women's experiences and women's culture. As a result, we may well write a conclusion that looks something like the following:

> As I have shown, both *Eastenders* and *Brookside* work within a broadly naturalistic framework that emphasizes social diversity (for example, the lesbian and gay characters, the limited presence of black and other minority ethnic groups) and that prioritizes the treatment of 'difficult' social issues (for example, domestic violence, HIV, drug use and unemployment): the 'gritty realism' of the programmes. We might assume that this emphasis on naturalism and social diversity would guarantee the programmes' popular appeal. However, as the essay has argued, *Coronation Street*'s appeal appears to lie, at least in part, precisely in its use of a diluted naturalism. It is far less concerned with representing a broad range of social issues and social groups, favouring instead an emphasis on strong female characters, story-lines that explore women's experience, and a rich array of comic characters and comic situations, many of which are at the expense of men. As the essay has argued, these aspects of *Coronation Street* can be said to connect with women's culture. The programme's women-centredness can thus be seen as a central part of its stronger position in the television ratings war.

If we break down this conclusion into its component parts, we can see that it does the following:

- recaps the key stages in the argument/summarizes the key debates raised by the question (that is, the argument that *Eastenders* and *Brookside* favour 'gritty realism' while *Coronation Street* is less naturalistic but strongly women-centred);
- provides a final condensed statement of the essay's core argument (this women-centredness underlies its popular appeal).

This conclusion hasn't identified absences in the argument that could be explored in future work, and it isn't always necessary to do this. However, we could have made a slightly stronger case for our position if we had said that *Coronation Street*'s women-centredness is *arguably* central to its popular appeal. We have shown that this *might* be the case but unless we can support this claim with research evidence it remains a hypothesis. As a result, we could have suggested that further research with *Coronation Street*'s audience is needed to substantiate our suggestion: an absence in our argument that could be explored in future work.

This, then, is one conclusion that we might have written to this particular essay question. However, you might disagree with the argument and want to write something completely different. Equally, you could have expressed the same points in a number of different ways. Alternatively, you might feel that you couldn't write a conclusion like this because it is 'too complicated' or 'too well written'. If this is the case, don't worry. You could write a serviceable conclusion in a much simpler form. The point is that there is more than one way to write a conclusion, and you should not view the *Coronation Street* example as a template to be followed slavishly.

## Summary ■■■■■■■■■■■■■■■■■■■■■■■■■■■■■■

- The primary job of a conclusion is to provide a final condensed version of your essay's core argument and thereby to summarize the key debates raised by the question, or provide an overview of 'current knowledge' on a given topic.

- Longer conclusions should: recap the subject of the essay in some form; recap the key stages in your argument/summarize the key debates raised by the question; provide a final condensed version of your argument that restates your position on the question; (if necessary) identify absences in your argument that could be explored in future work.

- By the end of a Level I course your conclusions should demonstrate the ability to summarize the content of the essay clearly and concisely. At Levels 2 and 3 you should move towards writing conclusions that emphasize sophisticated condensed versions of your core argument, and a sophisticated understanding of the key debates raised by the question.

- The conclusion should take up roughly 10 per cent of an essay.

# 8 References

Reference writing seems like time-consuming clerical activity, and it usually takes much longer than you could possibly imagine – so why do you have to do it?

## 8.1 Why are references needed?

There are several reasons why proper referencing is important. First, it demonstrates to those people who read your work – your tutors and examiners – that you are familiar with the key material on that topic and are knowledgeable about it. Secondly, it guards against plagiarism, since you must always acknowledge the source of any data or arguments you use which are not your own. Another reason for referencing is to allow the person who is reading your assignment to follow up any work you mention which sounds particularly interesting, or which they do not know. In order to do this the reader needs as much information as possible so he or she can find the work in a library or bookshop. Accurate referencing will also help you remember particular points, or pieces of work. Finally, an essay or project which is properly referenced looks like a professional piece of writing which is worthy of a further look. In short:

- References guarantee the 'authority' of your argument. They allow readers to check the accuracy of the claims that your essay makes.

- References allow the reader to look up a source or argument that they want to know more about.

- References act as a reminder to the author of sources used, and make it easier to follow up ideas at a later stage.

## 8.2 What should be referenced?

The following items need to be referenced:
- Quotations.
- Diagrams, statistical information or maps copied or cited in your essay.

- Work that is referred to but not quoted directly (for example, if you have written 'Several commentators have argued ...' or, 'Hall (1993) argues that ...' or, 'Research by Collins and Quillian (1969) suggests that ...').
- Otherwise unsubstantiated arguments and assertions (for example, if you have written, 'It is arguable that conventional notions of "normality" have been fundamentally challenged by the disability rights movement', you could then insert a reference or references that indicate to the reader that this idea has a considerable degree of academic respectability).

## 8.3  Writing references – basic principles

There are many ways to write references, but all have one feature in common: clear unambiguous details which allow someone to locate the work in a library or other source. Although in the OU you may find that some course teams have a preference for one system over another, almost all OU texts employ the Harvard system, so this is the system that we describe here. It is generally the easiest to use, so you can quickly get into the habit of referencing your work, and you will find it adequate for almost all purposes. It is certainly the method to start with.

### Abbreviated references

The Harvard system is clear and simple. Let's consider the basic principles as used for a book with a single author. Having written a quotation you simply add immediately after it an abbreviated reference; for example:

> The absolutist view of black and white cultures, as fixed, mutually impermeable expressions of racial and national identity, is a ubiquitous theme in 'common sense' (Gilroy, 1987, p.61).

Note that the full stop goes outside the bracket since the abbreviated reference is all part of the sentence. If you use the author's name in your sentence, you can also write your reference like this:

> Gilroy (1987, p.61) argues that forms of 'cultural absolutism' view black and white cultures as self-contained impermeable units.

It doesn't matter how you lay out the abbreviated reference as long as you are consistent and as long as it contains information in the following order:

- author's name;
- date of publication (make sure this is the date of the edition in your hand);
- if applicable (e.g. if using a direct quotation), the page number(s).

If you indent your examples, which is usual where quoted material is long, then you can dispose of opening and closing quotation marks. Your abbreviated reference should then fall in the line immediately following the quotation. All your abbreviated references must be expanded into full references in a list at the end of your essay.

### References in full

At the end of the essay, in a section entitled 'References', you need to write out all your references in full, organized alphabetically by authors' surnames. Let's consider first the Gilroy example above. In the full reference list the entry would be:

> Gilroy, P. (1987) *There Ain't No Black in the Union Jack*, London, Hutchinson.

This entry is typical of those for a book with a single author. All similar entries in the Harvard system should:

- begin with the author's surname and initial(s);
- give the date of publication (of the *relevant* edition);
- give the title of the work;
- give details of the place of publication and the publisher.

For books you won't need to include individual page numbers because you've given these to the reader already. Your references section will look similar to the one at the end of this book.

So much for a single author book, but things in life are rarely simple and references are no exception. You will find material quoted or referred to can come from different types of sources, and your reference list must reflect this. Unfortunately the basic referencing system needs a little more embellishment to cover the extra details for all but the most straightforward references. First, though, let's just note two more basic conventions which it is helpful to remember:

- titles of major works, programmes, etc. are set in italics or underlined;
- parts of works or minor works are put in single quotation marks.

We have listed in Appendix D examples of the reference types you are most likely to need. Even the most seasoned of academics find that they don't know these off by heart, so perhaps the best advice here is to try to remember the basic format and then look up the rest as you need them! Certainly you should not be intimidated by what looks like a complex process. Get started on the basics, using the guidance above and then simply remember to look up the embellishments as you need them. Note that by Level 3 you will be expected to include references correctly.

### Other conventions

Appendix E lists some abbreviations and foreign words in common use, including some frequently found in references. You are not expected to use all these conventions, but as your essay writing skills develop you may find some are quicker to use. If you do use them you must do so correctly.

You will see authors using a range of different formats and systems from the Harvard system, such as (for the abbreviated reference in the text): (Gilroy, 1987:61). You will also find authors using a footnote numbering system for the abbreviated reference, with the full reference at the bottom of the page or at the end of the text (this is the system used by Dyer quoted in Section 6.3 of this guide). Whatever the system, the general rules for what information is required are the same, only the layout is different.

## 8.4 When do you prepare the references?

It's a good idea to familiarize yourself with the basic principles for writing references as set out above before you begin your essay. Then, when you do begin, keep to hand Appendix D as you are researching your sources. Note down all the details you will require for your references. Almost all of us have at some time omitted to do this and learned how difficult it is to trace the reference details afterwards – usually at the very moment that the essay is ready to hand in.

## Summary ■ ■ ■ ■ ■ ■ ■ ■ ■ ■ ■ ■ ■ ■ ■ ■ ■ ■ ■ ■ ■ ■ ■ ■ ■ ■ ■ ■ ■ ■

- To write a reference using the Harvard system you should: give an abbreviated reference in the text; give a full reference in a 'References' section at the end of the text.

- Abbreviated references in the text are written : author's surname, publication date, page number(s) if applicable.

- Full references at the end of the text are written: (alphabetically by) author's surname and initials, publication date, place of publication and publisher.

- References to chapters in edited editions, to journal and newspaper articles, and various other sources are given in slightly different ways. Details of these are in Appendix D of this guide. Appendix E includes some abbreviations useful for references.

- Note down your reference details at the time you are finding your material.

- At Levels 1 and 2 you will be expected to learn how to provide references and begin to use them; at Level 3 you will be expected to reference as a matter of course.

■ ■ ■ ■ ■ ■ ■ ■ ■ ■ ■ ■ ■ ■ ■ ■ ■ ■ ■ ■ ■ ■ ■ ■ ■ ■ ■ ■ ■ ■ ■ ■ ■ ■ ■ ■

# 9 Some common worries

It is difficult to identify or predict all the worries that you may have in writing essays and where worries do arise we advise you to contact your tutor. But there are a few important points to know about and some things to avoid, so read this section carefully.

## 9.1 Plagiarism

Plagiarism means using someone else's work and passing it off as your own. It refers to copying other people's work word for word, or making only minor changes to it with the intention of representing it as your own. Attempting to gain credit for someone else's work is cheating, which risks incurring penalties (see *Student Handbook*, Section 9).

The problem with plagiarism (besides the fact that when done intentionally it is a form of cheating) is that it means that you probably have not thoroughly understood what you've written about. The process of putting arguments into your own words is a crucial part of grasping ideas and committing them to memory. It also helps you to learn how to use and apply the ideas *for yourself.* Plagiarism, if nothing else, is thus a waste of your time. If you are in any doubt about how to avoid plagiarism you should check with your tutor. Essays which contain plagiarized work will attract fail grades.

Of course, the problem is how to avoid plagiarizing in the first place. A lot of people plagiarize unintentionally. This can occur because of:

- *Bad note taking*
  Sometimes you may find yourself copying chunks of the course for your notes and then failing to put this in quotation marks, or sometimes paraphrase from course materials in your notes without putting the argument in your own words. This will then appear in the essay as an argument that bears a remarkable similarity to a paragraph in the course.
- *Lack of confidence*
  If an argument is very complex or you are particularly unclear about it, you may stick to the course material as closely as

possible so you don't 'get it wrong' or because of a feeling that the words could not be improved upon. The problem is that your tutor won't be able to tell whether you've understood the argument or not since you won't have reproduced it in your own terms.

To avoid unintentional plagiarism, adopt good note-taking habits, ask your tutor or other students if you don't understand something, and re-read your essays before submitting them. Tutors can usually spot plagiarism because the style or tone of the writing will suddenly change. If you re-read your essays you will notice when this happens as well.

Occasionally some people will deliberately plagiarize an essay. As indicated above, this is a serious offence, since it is a form of academic theft. In the case of assessed course work, it is also an attempt to gain qualifications by cheating, and this will incur such penalties as the University may determine. If you are tempted to plagiarize because you are having problems with the course or have fallen behind with your work, telephone your OU tutor or seek OU counselling help instead. They will help you identify a much better solution to the problem.

## 9.2  Writing too much

As you will know, OU essays have word limits. Many students point out that they could easily write a whole lot more on any one topic. Indeed, people write 80,000 word books on the sort of issues that you address in your essays, so everyone knows that word limits can be rather restrictive. However, they are not set merely to irritate you. Shorter essays are an important academic tool. In writing them, you learn how to prioritize and select material, and how to condense big topics into a punchy, easily digested form. These are academic skills that you will need even in writing much longer pieces of work. We know that it's painful but, if you're writing too much, be ruthless. Concentrate on the biggest, most important arguments and examples and cut the rest. Your work will almost certainly be better for it. You need to remember that some course teams instruct tutors to deduct marks for an over-long essay. Furthermore, some tutors may feel that writing over length allows you to cover a topic in more detail than other people and thus confers an unfair advantage on you.

## 9.3 Using the 'I' word

Many tutors will tell you not to use 'I' in your essays (for example, not to write 'In this essay I intend to explore ...'). This is because 'I' is sometimes thought to indicate a lack of objectivity. In any case, you can often avoid personal pronouns completely (for example, by writing 'This essay will explore ...'). This latter style is what you should aim to adopt as you progress from Level 1 to Levels 2 and 3. However, different disciplines within the social sciences have different practices concerning the use of personal pronouns, and so it is always a good idea to check with your course tutor what is expected for any particular course. While it is true that there are no hard and fast rules about using 'I' in social sciences essays, there are well established 'customs and practices'.

## 9.4 Using your own experiences

Some essay questions will ask you to draw on personal experiences, and sometimes you may want to include personal experiences to illustrate an argument or to grab the reader's attention. It may be particularly useful to do this if you have personal experience of the topic under discussion (for example, if you work in the field). Used carefully, personal experience can provide an excellent source of evidence, and course material can sometimes be remembered more easily when tied to personal or local experience. However, there is a danger that personal experiences will sound like 'bar room philosophy': little more than unsubstantiated personal opinion. Thus, if you use personal experience you will need to demonstrate clearly how and why it is relevant to both the question and the course, and be able to substantiate any claims that you make on the basis of it.

## 9.5 Using sources other than OU course materials

Some OU courses ask you to explore non-course material as part of your work. However, except where you are explicitly asked to do this, you are not expected to do extra (that is, non-course) reading for your essays. You are assessed and examined on the course as it stands, so bringing in additional material isn't necessary. Having said this, you might know of or have read something that is particularly relevant to the question and which you feel adds significantly to your answer. If this is the case then include it. However, as is made clear in one course's skills booklet (Brook, 1987), make sure that it relates directly to the themes of the course and that it is not used at the expense of the course's own examples and arguments.

## 9.6 Presentation, spelling and grammar

OU essays are marked on their content, not on the beauty of their presentation, but remember that presentation may affect your reader's interpretation of the content.

Your essay will need to be neat enough to read (you can write it long hand, type it or word process it), but nothing more is expected of you. When submitting an assignment all you need is your PT3 (the cover sheet) and the essay itself, so unless presentation folders and plastic envelopes make you feel particularly good, you don't need to worry about them. The one luxury you might extend yourself is a paper-clip or preferably a stapler, since this will prevent pages getting detached and lost.

Spelling, grammar and punctuation are more important issues. The baseline here is that essays should be readable and make sense. Your spelling, grammar and punctuation need to be good enough to communicate effectively to your reader and, at degree level or equivalent, this implies the ability to write with only minor imperfections in each area. If you have difficulty with spelling, grammar or punctuation we suggest that you seek the advice of your tutor.

Choose your words appropriately and correctly. Use of jargon words has already been mentioned in Section 6.4 'Clear sentences and paragraphs'. If you use abbreviations or foreign words make sure you use them correctly (Appendix E has a list of those commonly found).

Finally, the OU offers general guidelines on basic layout. These are:

- write on one side of A4 paper;
- write your name, the assignment number and your personal identifier at the top of the first sheet, and the assignment number and your personal identifier on all subsequent sheets;
- write out the question at the start of the essay;

- leave a margin of about one-and-a-half inches on the left of the page and about one inch at the bottom (if you don't do this your tutor will have to write over your script);
- remember to number your pages.

## 9.7  English as a first language

In common with many other higher education institutions, the OU tends to assume that you use standard English. This includes essay writing, and standard English is therefore the only language currently accepted in social sciences assignments.

## 9.8  Extensions

OU policy is that essays should be submitted by the cut-off date specified on your course calendar. It is important to submit assignments on time for the following reasons:

- it's very easy to fall behind!
- taking extra time over an essay, unless you have good reason for late submission, gives you an unfair advantage over other people on your course;
- taking extra time can provide, or be seen to provide, an opportunity to cheat by reading other students' work.

However, most tutors will be happy to give you an extension under specific circumstances. For example:

- if you or someone close to you has been ill and this has interrupted your work;
- if your OU work has been disrupted by other exceptional or unforeseen problems, for example in your paid work or at home;
- if you are having significant problems with the course itself and you have discussed these with your tutor.

Extensions should always be arranged with your tutor in advance of the TMA cut-off date, and you should note that there is no late submission allowed for the final assignment. You should also note that there are OU regulations regarding more than two extensions per full credit course. (See the *Student Handbook*, Section 9, for full details of late submission.)

# Summary ■ ■ ■ ■ ■ ■ ■ ■ ■ ■ ■ ■ ■ ■ ■ ■ ■ ■ ■ ■ ■ ■ ■ ■ ■ ■ ■ ■ ■ ■ ■ ■

- Plagiarism means copying someone else's work and claiming it as your own. Plagiarized essays will attract a fail grade. Deliberate plagiarism which constitutes cheating will result in disciplinary action.

- Plagiarism is often unintentional. To avoid this make sure that you write essay notes in your own words and always put quotations in quotation marks or indent the text; re-read your essays, looking for sudden changes in style or tone; clarify difficult points with your tutor or fellow students so that you can reproduce them in your own words.

- Writing to a word limit is an important academic skill: it teaches you to condense complex material into its components parts, and to select and communicate core arguments.

- Personal experiences can be a useful source of evidence, and some courses require you to use them. However, be careful to relate these to the course and the essay question and to substantiate your claims.

- Some OU courses require you to explore non-course material in your work. Except in these instances, you will be marked on your understanding of the course as it stands. If you know of additional material, its relevance should be clearly established and it should not be included at the expense of arguments or evidence from the course itself.

- Essays are expected to be readable, and by Level 2 and 3 show a solid grasp of standard English, spelling, punctuation and grammar. They can be hand written, typed or word processed.

- Extensions are available on OU courses in cases of sickness or other serious disruption to your work. They should be asked for in advance.

■ ■ ■ ■ ■ ■ ■ ■ ■ ■ ■ ■ ■ ■ ■ ■ ■ ■ ■ ■ ■ ■ ■ ■ ■ ■ ■ ■ ■ ■ ■ ■ ■ ■ ■ ■ ■ ■ ■ ■ ■ ■ ■

# 10 Concluding remarks

Having submitted your essay, what next? First, enjoy briefly that 'It's done!' euphoria. Then, if you have not already done so, and before you are expecting your marked essay to come back, read through the advice in Appendix A 'What to do when your essay comes back'. Keep your recorded key points of feedback ready to pick up again when you are working on your next essay ...

Writing academic essays in the social sciences is probably very different from any other writing you have done before. But it is central to getting a degree. It is hoped that by knowing what is required, and the techniques that help, you will not only feel more at ease writing your TMAs but will be able to demonstrate your knowledge and understanding to maximum effect. Hopefully, you will find this guide a valuable resource which will help you well on your way to *Good essay writing*!

## Appendix A

# *What to do when your essay comes back*

*Maggie Coats*

If you're like most other people, when you get an essay back you'll check the grade first, read the comments on the PT3 (the cover sheet), and quickly flip through the rest looking for any major embarrassments. You'll probably read it with more care only if the tutor has written something particularly complimentary or irritating. However, learning from previous pieces of writing is an important way of building on your writing skills. Maggie Coats is an Associate Lecturer in the OU and here are her suggestions for learning from your last essay:

- Take a quick look at the score and PT3, feel pleased, angry or despairing, depending on your grade/mood, then put the essay aside until you are ready to look at it with a more 'objective' eye.
- Give yourself twenty to thirty minutes to look over the essay in detail.
- Re-read the PT3 comments and note the main points.
- Re-read the essay itself, including the tutor's comments; mark your responses to these comments. Do you agree or disagree? Is there anything you don't understand?
- Next, re-read the PT3. Can you see what the tutor is saying?
- Do you agree with the grade? If not, make a note of it and raise this with your tutor. Is there anything that you still don't understand? Make a note and ask your tutor.
- On a separate sheet, write down one or two key points that will improve your performance when writing the next assignment. File these.

Source: adapted from Coats, undated, Handout Material 2.

# Appendix B

# *Process and command words in essay questions*

*Sue Cole and Pauline Harris*

Sue Cole and Pauline Harris, both OU Associate Lecturers, offer the following explanations for the command words that you're likely to find in essay questions.

| | |
|---|---|
| Account for | Explain, clarify, give reasons for. |
| Analyse | Resolve into its component parts. Examine critically or minutely. |
| Assess | Determine the value of, weigh up (see also Evaluate). |
| Compare | Look for similarities and differences between, perhaps reach conclusions about which is preferable and justify this clearly. |
| Contrast | Set in opposition in order to bring out the differences sharply. |
| Compare and contrast | Find some points of common ground between x and y and show where or how they differ. |
| Criticize | Make a judgement (backed by a discussion of the evidence or reasoning involved) about the merit of theories or opinions or about the truth of facts. |
| Define | State the exact meaning of a word or phrase. In some cases it may be necessary or desirable to examine different possible or often used definitions. |
| Describe | Give a detailed account of … |
| Discuss | Explain, then give two sides of the issue and any implications. |
| Distinguish or differentiate between | Look for differences between … |
| Evaluate | Make an appraisal of the worth/validity/effectiveness of something in the light of its truth or usefulness (see also Assess). |

| | |
|---|---|
| Examine the argument that … | Look in detail at this line of argument. |
| Explain | Give details about how and why it is … |
| How far … | To what extent … Usually involves looking at evidence/arguments for and against and weighing them up. |
| Illustrate | Make clear and explicit, usually requires the use of carefully chosen examples. |
| Justify | Show adequate grounds for decisions or conclusions, answer the main objections likely to be made about them. |
| Outline | Give the main features or general principles of a subject, omitting minor details and emphasizing structure and arrangement. |
| State | Present in a brief, clear way. |
| Summarize | Give a concise, clear explanation or account of … presenting the chief factors and omitting minor details and examples (see also Outline). |
| What arguments can be made for and against the view that … | Look at both sides of this argument. |

Source: adapted from Cole and Harris, undated, Handout Material 2.

## Appendix C

# *Brainstorming: producing a 'mind map'*

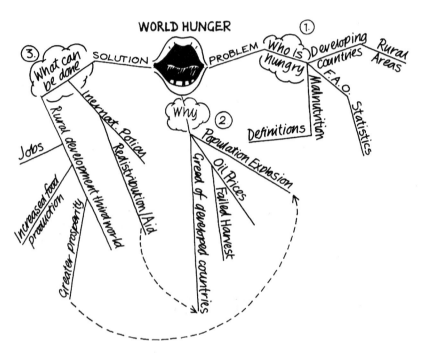

Source: P.N.L. Study Guides, 1992.

## Appendix D

# *Preparing different types of references*

## Books

### Single author

Just to recap, abbreviated references (including the example in Section 8.3): '(Gilroy, 1987, p.61)' and '(Barker, 1981, p.36)' would in the reference list be (alphabetically by surname):

Barker, M. (1981) The New Racism, London, Junction Books.

Gilroy, P. (1987) *There Ain't No Black in the Union Jack*, London, Hutchinson.

Sometimes one author will be cited from more than one work in the same publication year; in this case the abbreviated reference would be: '(Hall, 1994a)' and '(Hall, 1994b)' and you would then list them in the references with the 1994a entry followed by 1994b. (The order of 'a' and 'b' can be according to the order in which they occur in the book or arranged alphabetically by title, but whichever you chose be consistent!)

### More than one author

Where there are two authors, the form for the abbreviated reference should be '(Barrett and McIntosh, 1982)' and in the references list:

Barrett, M. and McIntosh, M. (1982) *The Anti-Social Family*, London, Verso.

Where there are three or more authors, the abbreviated reference gives only the first author then 'et al.' (meaning 'and others'): '(Kinsey et al., 1986, pp.36–49)'. The reference list gives the names of all the authors in the order in which they appear in the work itself:

Kinsey, R., Lea, J. and Young, J. (1986) *Losing the Fight against Crime*, Oxford, Basil Blackwell.

If you have more than one author to reference in one citation, list them alphabetically in the text: for example, '(Barker, 1981; Gilroy, 1987)'.

### Edited collections

These refer to a collection of articles or extracts compiled by one or more editors.

If you simply refer to the book itself, note the name(s) of the editor(s) as if they were the author; the abbreviated reference '(Epstein, 1994)', for example, would have this reference list entry:

> Epstein, D. (ed.) (1994) *Challenging Lesbian and Gay Inequalities in Education*, Buckingham, Open University Press.

If you are quoting from one of the articles/extracts, the abbreviated reference should give the name(s) of the author(s) of that article/extract and the date of the edited collection: '(Mac an Ghaill, 1994)'. The full reference will have both the names of the author(s) and the editor(s) thus:

> Mac an Ghaill, M. (1994) '(In)visibility: sexuality, race and masculinity in the school context' in Epstein, D. (ed.) *Challenging Lesbian and Gay Inequalities in Education*, Buckingham, Open University Press.

## An author quoted in another text

Assuming that the work of the quoted author is not available, follow the basic principles: so, for example, an abbreviated reference '(Billingsley, quoted in Dawson and Kennedy-Skipton, 1968)' would have as its full reference:

> Dawson, G. and Kennedy-Skipton, L. (1968) *Elizabethan Handwriting*, London, Faber & Faber.

See also below for an author quoted or referred to in Open University material.

## Journal articles

If the article you are referring to or quoting from appears in a journal, the abbreviated reference takes the usual format: '(Gallie, 1994)'. In the full reference you include details of the volume/number and page numbers, but you don't include place of publication or publisher's name. For example:

> Gallie, D. (1994) 'Are the unemployed an underclass? Some evidence from the social change and economic life initiative', *Sociology*, vol.28, no.3, pp.737–58.

## Newspaper articles

These follow much the same pattern as journal articles. An abbreviated reference would be '(Kelsay and Rowe, 1990)' and its full reference would have the date of publication at the end:

> Kelsay, T. and Rowe, T. (1990) 'Academics "were funded by racist American trust"', *Independent on Sunday*, 1 March.

## Open University courses/course material

For OU course material, the Open University is usually considered the author, so text including an abbreviated reference would be: 'Rogers expresses the view that … (The Open University, 1993, p.37)'. The full reference can be a little tricky for the name of the work (your tutor can advise you on possible shortened forms) but here's one full example:

> The Open University (1993) D211 *Social Problems and Social Welfare*, Block 3 *Private Troubles and Public Issues*, 2nd edn, Milton Keynes, The Open University.

In recent years the OU has started publishing its course materials (particularly in social sciences) in collaboration with other publishers. In such courses there are frequently cross-references between the books of each course, and in these cases the authors, chapters and books are referenced in exactly the same way as non-OU materials. For example, a chapter written by OU academic John Muncie for the course D315 *Crime, Order and Society* would be referenced as follows:

> Muncie, J. (1996) 'The construction and deconstruction of crime', in Muncie, J. and McLaughlin, E. (eds.) *The Problem of Crime*, London, Sage/The Open University.

### An author quoted/referred to in Open University course material

Much of what you might quote from or refer to may have been written by authors cited in the OU course you are studying. If you recycle a quotation (or similarly make reference to an author's work) you should acknowledge that this is 'quoted in' such-and-such a course. Let's consider an example.

You might decide to quote the following extract quoted in Unit 20 of D211: 'in practice community care equals care by the family, and in practice care by the family equals care by women', which comes from page 494 of an article by Finch and Groves in the *Journal of Social Policy*. Your abbreviated reference would be: (Finch and Groves, 1980, p.494) and the full reference:

> Finch, J. and Groves, D. (1980) 'Community care and the family: a case for equal opportunities', *Journal of Social Policy*, vol.9, no.4, quoted in The Open University (1988) D211 *Social Problems and Social Welfare*, Block 3 *Private Troubles and Public Issues*, Unit 20, Milton Keynes, The Open University.

(Here it would certainly be helpful if you agreed a much shorter version with your tutor; you could, for instance, consider omitting all italicized OU titles.)

It is just as likely that you will decide to refer to the Finch and Groves article without quoting from them directly. This moves you into something of a grey referencing area. Should you reference sources as though you have gone to the original text and read them, or should you reference the course materials? Strictly speaking, assuming that Loney is the OU author, you should write something like: 'Loney argues that researchers like Finch and Grove (1980) have suggested that community care most often equals care by women (The Open University, 1988)'. You could then reference both sources in your references list, but in practice most tutors would be happy with you writing the more direct 'Finch and Grove argue that community care most often equals care by women (Finch and Grove, 1980)'. The full reference would then be as noted above (or an acceptable shortened version of it).

## Personal communication

If you quote something said in a conversation or letter, you should note this: '(Archer, 1994, personal conversation with author)'. You may or may not need to include this in the references list, but if you do you should add the initials to the reference entry there.

## Cassettes, television, radio programmes and other electronic media

You could first discuss with your tutor whether adequate information provided in the body of your essay could avoid the need to include this material in your reference list. Full references for these media will vary, but the most important thing is that your reader is readily able to trace the source of cited material from the information you supply.

You are most likely to refer to or quote from OU-produced non-print media. Make this similar to OU print material. For example, for an OU TV programme you would have in the text: (The Open University, 1994). The full reference would read:

> The Open University (1994) D103 *Society and Social Science: A Foundation Course*, TV 10 *Questions of National Identity*, Milton Keynes, The Open University.

The full reference for a cassette would give the publication date of the tape (printed on the cassette) and the other details similar to those for OU printed material:

> The Open University (1997) D316 *Democracy: from Classical Times to the Present*, Tape 2264, Side 2, 'Citizenship and civil liberty', Milton Keynes, The Open University.

Follow similar formats for non-OU material. No firm guidelines for referencing electronic sources such as CD-ROM or World Wide Web (WWW) have yet been established, but if you ever want to refer to these you must include, in addition to as much of the above information as is available, the medium (such as CD-ROM), and in the case of WWW the address and date of 'visit' to the site.

## Identifying the details for references

Publication details are given near the front of the book on the 'imprint' page, which usually comes after the title page. Please check carefully the particular notes for each component (date, edition, place, publisher).

### Different publication dates

The date of publication you need is the latest year noted in the book that you have. For instance, *German Ideology*, a key text in classical Marxist theory, first appeared in the nineteenth century. However, our copy was published in 1974. This reference will read:

> Marx, K. and Engels, F. (1974) *German Ideology*, London, Lawrence and Wishart.

Where dates for reprints are noted, use the year given against the copyright (©) line.

### Retaining early publication dates

For quoted material from a very early work, where you want to include the early date but your quotation is from a modern reproduction, note the later date first, separated from the original date by a slash. For example, for *Origin of Species by Means of Natural Selection*, the abbreviated reference would be: '(Darwin, 1997/1859, p.23)'; and the full reference would include the date: '(1997/1859)'.

## Edition numbers

Books are not only reprinted but they can be revised and republished as a new *edition*. This often occurs when new material is added because the book has become dated. In fact, our 1974 copy of *German Ideology* is the second edition of this particular version of the book. A first edition was published in 1970. Because second and subsequent editions contain alterations, it is important to tell the reader which version you're working from. This reference should therefore read:

> Marx, K. and Engels, F. (1974) *German Ideology*, 2nd edn, London, Lawrence and Wishart.

## Publisher and place of publication

Assuming that you are writing in Britain or for a British audience, you need to quote the British place of publication of British publishers. For example, Routledge is based in London, so you put London as the place of publication; Open University Press (a company separate from the Open University itself) is based in Buckingham, so you put Buckingham. However, some books that you reference may be published overseas and imported into Britain. In such cases you need to indicate that the book is an overseas publication.

Be sure to give the place of publication (that is, the city or town where the publisher is based) and not the place where the book was printed.

## Collaborative publishing

Sometimes books are brought out by more than one publisher. As noted above, OU course books are often collaborations of this kind. In such cases, name both publishers. The place of publication will be indicated on the imprint page. An abbreviated reference could be '(Goodman and Graddol, 1994)'. It would carry the full reference:

> Goodman, S. and Graddol, D. (eds) (1996) *Redesigning English: New Texts, New Identities*, London, Routledge/The Open University.

## Appendix E

# *Abbreviations and words in foreign languages*

At various points in your reading, especially in references, you will come across various abbreviations or words written in foreign languages. You may need to use these in your own writing, so here's a list of some of the more common examples.

| | |
|---|---|
| cf. (*confer*) | compare |
| ch., chs, (or chap., chaps) | chapter(s) |
| ed., eds | editor(s) |
| edn | edition |
| e.g. (*exempli gratia*) | an easy one: 'for example' (not to be confused with 'i.e.') |
| et al. (*et alia*) | 'and others', used for multiple authors as in '(Hatt et al., 1978)' |
| *et seq.* (*et sequens*) | 'and the following' (for example, pp.16 *et seq.*) |
| ff. | alternative to *et seq.* (for example, pp.16 ff.) |
| ibid. (*ibidem*) | 'in the same work' (as the last reference). Used in footnotes/endnotes to save writing out the whole reference again (for example, Gilroy, ibid. p.61). |
| i.e. (*id est*) | an easy one: 'that is' (not to be confused with 'e.g.') |
| loc. cit. (*loco citato*) | 'in the same place' (as the previous passage) |
| n., nn. | note(s), as in 'p.4, n.2' |
| op. cit. (*opere citato*) | 'in the work recently cited' as in 'Gilroy, op. cit., p.67'; used in footnotes/endnotes to save writing a full reference for a work previously cited, but not the last reference (cf. 'ibid.') |
| *passim* | throughout the work (not on one page only) |
| p., pp. | page, pages |
| q.v. (*quod vide*) | 'which see' (for cross-referencing) |
| (s*ic*) | 'thus'; indicates that questionable/apparently incorrect quoted material is faithfully reproduced from the original |
| trans., tr. | translator |
| vol., vols | volume(s) |

## Appendix F

# *Using a Word Processor to Write (or Grow) an Essay*

*Andy Sutton*

(Andy Sutton is an Associate Lecturer with the OU.)

## I Introduction

This is intended as a guide for students who do, or wish to, write essays on a word processor (WP). Whatever your reason for using one, it is best to get the most out of the machine; it can do much more than make your work look neat.

It is not a technical guide in the sense of using the computer hardware or software, but should help you to use the potential of a WP so that it is not simply treated as a typewriter. Effective use of a WP can speed up the essay writing process, and can help to develop a good discipline of planning.

My early experience was of getting an essay into a fairly advanced stage on paper before plugging in the WP, sometimes just typing out a finished version. I have discovered that by involving the WP at an early stage I can 'grow' the essay so that a basic plan evolves into the essay on screen. What I hope to do is show by example how a WP can be used, by dealing with an actual essay and explaining the stages of development.

Briefly, I start on the WP with an essay plan, and gradually replace each bit of the plan, on screen, with the paragraph or section which it represents. This is what I mean by 'growing' an essay. When I am half-way through you would see an odd mix of polished text and half baked notes. There are no 'best' ways to use a WP. Please use the ideas flexibly. This is a method which suits me, experience will help you to find one which suits you.

Most of the advice given here can be followed with any word processor. Some of the more exotic features such as grammar checking will not be available in all packages, but the features needed for 'growing' an essay are present in even the simplest and most inexpensive processors.

## 2  Do you have green fingers?

Using the WP successfully probably requires reasonable keyboard skills. Don't let this put you off. I have got away with two-finger typing for ages, and I am now quite fast. However if you are starting out, and might want to use a WP for some time to come, think about learning to type properly. There are courses, software, or books which will help. In the meantime you have an essay to write …

The best way (indeed the only way) to speed up your typing is practice. You may want to get reasonably familiar with a keyboard before starting to delve into these techniques.

## 3  Preparing the ground

The title I am using as an illustration is: Does Father Christmas really exist?

While preparing I make notes by hand (I would not advise doing this on the WP unless you have to). I don't need to worry if I'm away from my machine, and in any case I like to have my notes spread around me while I am planning, which would mean printing them out before using them if they existed only on a disc.

The next stage I also do by hand. I brainstorm on all the things which I might want to include in the essay. This process produces a sheet of ideas which are in a rather random order.

The next stage will be producing a plan on the WP which is an ordered and refined version of the sheet I have just produced, so there is a case for doing the brainstorming on the WP, and then simply moving it around and changing it on screen. Personally, I don't do that because cutting and pasting very short phrases seems like a lot of bother. However you should see how it works for you. If you are using a system which allows you to see and manipulate two documents at the same time (eg WordPerfect) you could brainstorm onto one screen, then copy across into the other to get them in order. 'Drag and Drop' facilities in Windows or Mac systems may make on-screen manipulation more attractive.

# 4 Planting the seeds

At this stage then I have a sheet of ideas which will become a plan. I have some general idea of my strategy and some thoughts about my answer to the question, based on my reading and thinking so far.

My aim with a plan is to produce a list of short phrases, or sometimes just single words, each of which captures an idea which will eventually be turned into a paragraph. So in theory, fifteen words or phrases will turn into fifteen paragraphs which is the finished essay.

It doesn't always work out like that. Sometimes a phrase becomes a couple or more paragraphs when I think about it further while writing. Also, sometimes when I am doing the plan an idea will form in my head which I think is well expressed, so I write a few sentences so that I don't lose it. Often these sentences will still be present in the final essay. I think it is wise to follow your instincts at this planning stage, rather than sticking rigidly to a formula.

So in my head at this moment is some idea that I have to show why I think Father Christmas does exist, and my main argument is that the alternative theories are less credible. Of course before I can write my argument I need to explain about Father Christmas and a few other things. All this is on my mind as I formulate the plan.

It would probably be worth reading the finished essay now so that you will see how the essay and plan are related, or else this plan will look fairly nonsensical. The essay is printed at the very end of this appendix.

# 5 The green shoots

*Plan:*

*Does Father Christmas really exist?*

*introduction*

*definitions*

*can't prove be seeing, sack of cinders*

*quote from Rudolph*

*must be somebody magic, chimney blocked, no chimney etc*

*look at alternative*

*it cannot be your parents. My Mum lives eighty miles away, and has arthritis, so the idea that she travels to my house in the middle of the night and climbs up on the roof (ladder locked up) and then drops down the chimney to bring my present seems much more unlikely than ...*

*arguments used against Father Christmas: different in diff shops countered by considering other people dressing up. Eg of Hitler*

*weigh up evidence*

*conclusion*

The plan is not always typed in order. I put a few bits in, the definitions, for instance, are vital and fixed. Then I start to key in the other bits as I think of them. These will not be in order, but I insert them as I see fit, so that they end up in order on the screen, aiming all the time for the whole thing to flow and build up. Some moving around goes on, using 'cut and paste' facilities.

You will see from the plan that some ideas are much better developed than others. Also, though there is none here, it is not unusual to have bits in the plan which end up being ditched.

## 6 Feeding and watering

Now the plan needs to be turned into an essay which can be handed in. You may want to print out your plan, or keep it as a separate document on screen, to refer to while you 'grow' the real thing. Personally, I don't do that.

What I do is to go through from beginning to end expanding each part of the plan into fully and properly written text.

What I do with each part depends on how developed it already is. With something like 'quote from Rudolph' I start typing above it, so that I can still see it on screen as I am typing the full paragraph. When I have done that paragraph I delete that part of the plan.

A more developed section, such as the one about my Mum, tends to be just added to as it is, that is, I type around it.

It would be nice if you could just work through the essay from beginning to end and emerge with a final product. What I usually find is that I think of something new to add to the plan part-way through another paragraph, so I go to that section and add it before I lose it. Or I think of something I should have put in earlier on a section I thought I had finished, so I go back and add it. Sometimes I change my mind about the order of paragraphs, and swap a couple around or move one to a different place altogether. The beauty of a WP is that it allows you to do this simply.

I find it better to build up the reference section as I go along. When I quote or refer to a work, I whiz to the end of the document and type in the full reference (inserting if necessary to keep the references in alphabetical order). This is much easier than trying to find them all and add them at the end. you may also have a sort function on your WP which can get them in alphabetical order for you.

Remember, you can write notes to yourself as you go along. You simply delete them afterwards. Make sure you can spot them though. For this (according to which WP you have) you could underline, alternate screen colour, key in stars or other non-text character, or even use the comments facility. Choose anything that you can spot quickly and that you can easily search for. I often use stars, and do something like:

****remember to find this reference

Then I can use 'search' facilities to find all the instances of four stars, check that I've done whatever it is, and delete the comments.

## 7 Weeding

You now have a first draft. There will be bits to add, change or what-have-you, but again on the WP this is easy. Some people feel that they can spot mistakes more easily on printed paper than on screen, so you might want to print out your draft. Similarly, it sometimes easier to 'see' the overall structure on pages which you can lay before you rather than scrolling your essay through the 'window' of a screen.

## 8 Useful tools

Here are some of the WP features which I find most useful. I'm sure most WP software has these. Some will have additional ones that are useful. Explore your manual, or find other users of your software, to pick up other good tips.

## Copy/cut/paste

These are the functions which allow you to move bits of text around, so that you don't have to delete something and retype it just because you change your mind about where it ought to be. In a Windows or Apple Mac system you can often 'drag and drop' with a mouse, which achieves the same thing.

## Stored phrases

This is the option to use a single key to type in a whole phrase and they can be stored as 'macros'. My feeling is that there aren't many word combinations which occur often enough in academic essays to make storing them worthwhile. However, sometimes there is one which is going to come up a lot in one particular essay, so it might be worth making it a temporary phrase, eg 'petite bourgeoisie'. I don't do this though for just one essay. I use EXCHANGE (see below). On the Amstrad all temporary stored phrases are lost when you switch off the machine, which means if you don't do the complete essay in one session you have to re-enter them every time. In WordPerfect you could store them on disk, but unless you are very methodical and delete them after use you will have lots of mostly useless macros building up.

Perhaps more useful, particularly on the Amstrad PCWs, is using stored phrases to store codes for titles. When stored in a phrase in your preferred combination these are quite convenient to use.

## Exchange or REPLACE

This is the option which seeks all occurrences of a work or phrase in the document, and swaps them for something else.

I use this to help with a long or difficult phrase or word which is going to occur a lot in an essay. For example, 'humanistic psychology'. What I do is to type 'HP' instead all the way through, then at the end swap all the 'HP's' for the real thing using EXCHANGE. Remember to use a combination of letters which is not likely to occur elsewhere, or you might end up with 'TOOThumanistic psychologyICK'.

Be careful with 'exchange' options. Some versions look only for whole words, but if not it is wise to include spaces around your search word. If you wanted to change all occurrences of 'cat' to 'feline' you could end up talking about a 'felinech 22 situation'. This is avoided if you exchange '[SPACE]cat[SPACE]' for '[SPACE]feline[SPACE]'. though it will miss 'cats' so you might have to run it again to get the plurals. You should use a 'confirm each exchange' option if you have one.

## Spell checkers

Spell checkers are useful, but must be used with care. They should add to, not replace, human checking.

The problem with the electronic checkers is that they know how words are spelled, but not what words mean, so they let you get away with things like:

> Here care is four sail butt my fiend does know won't two by it.

when you mean:

> Her car is for sale but my friend does not want to buy it.

All the mistakes are genuine words, but not the ones intended. A spell checker would not find any errors.

They also do nothing about poor grammar. It is always worth reading through for errors yourself, or getting a friend (or fiend?) to check for you.

## Grammar checkers

Later versions of WordPerfect include grammar checking, and there are several other packages available. At their present state of development I think they are of limited use because they are slow and produce a lot of false alarms and miss genuine errors. In time they may become more useful. If you have one, have a try and see if you find the results worth the effort and time.

My grammar checker found only two problems with the 'My care is four sal butt my fiend does knot wont two by it.' sentence, the 'butt' and 'wont'. Everything else is passed through. Its suggested replacement for 'wont' was 'wont' not 'want', and the advice for 'butt' I didn't understand.

They are quite good at finding long sentences, and commenting on your writing style.

## Page layout, headers and footers

If you haven't already, it is worth setting up a standard document format for your essays. In WordPerfect use the style library facility for this or (my preference) record a macro which makes the adjustments for you. In Locoscript use a 'template.std'. If you don't know how to do these things, do you have a friend who could set them up for you? Once set up, they are very easy to use.

Your layout should follow any rules about margin sizes, etc, and you can use the facility to automatically print things at the tops and bottoms of pages (headers and footers) to include the page numbers, your name, course and personal identifier on each page.

## Word counters

For assessed essays it is very useful to be able to count words quickly and accurately, because you are normally working to word limits. The time to use this feature is not when you have produced your first draft and you want to know how far out you have drifted, but after each sub-section of your essay. If your counter will count specific sections of text then this is perfect.

With this facility you really can 'grow' your essay. With a little planning you can decide how long each section ought to be before you write any of it. You could include this information in your plan on the WP. Then you can monitor the length of the essay as it progresses. For example, you might decide that 100 words is the most you can allow for the introduction,. So, when you have written your introduction, and it is 150 words long, you can decide whether to juggle the rest to accommodate the extra (dangerous : you might go over elsewhere too) or start chopping something out straight away (safer). If you do this for each section it is much better than finishing a 1000 word essay and finding it is 500 words too long. I think this kind of length planning is a good discipline to foster, and the WP facilitates it.

## Line numbering

this option lets you add numbers down the left margin of your page. These can be useful for a tutor to refer to sections when marking. This is especially useful if the tutor gives comments on a separate piece of paper rather than writing on your script. The tutor can say 'page 2 line 15' rather than 'page 2 the bit where you define ...'

Eventually you will get a feel for the package which you use. For example, get to know how many words (roughly) fit on a page. I usually find that a thousand words takes up about 8K on disk. These rules of thumb can be useful.

# 9 Style

In replacing handwriting with standardized printing, WPs are hacking away at individual style. I do not wish to compound this, but a couple of conventions of presentation might be useful. Many WP manuals do not give advice about typing, and if you are self taught, like me, you may miss these points:

a.  It is normal to leave a space after a comma and a full stop.

b.  It is not fashionable to indent the first word of a paragraph. If you find your paragraphs are not clearly differentiated, the normal alternative is to leave a line between them.

# 10 Pests and diseases

- There is a danger of which a word processing student may need to be aware. This is that getting too used to a keyboard may be a problem at exam time if you have got to write by hand (which is likely to be the case for most students). To counter this I recommend extensive hand-writing practice from revision time onwards. Do not be tempted to plan possible exam answers on the WP, do it by hand. Get used to doing all your planning and writing in exam type conditions using an old fashioned pen and paper.

- Word processors are supposed to be moving us towards a paperless environment. Anyone who uses one regularly will confirm that the opposite is true. Please spare a thought for the environment, don't print out lots of unnecessary drafts and copies.

- A note on loss and safety. Properly backed up disc copies can be stored in different locations (to minimize the risk from theft and fire), and easily updated. They are inherently safer than paper copies as well as cheaper and 'greener'. However, this does reply on you having a proper backup procedure, and using it diligently. People do lose work on WPs, but it is easy not to if you follow the rules.

# 11 The Harvested Crop

## Does Father Christmas really exist?

In this essay I will argue that Father Christmas does exist. To support this I will show that there is some evidence in favour of his existence, but the main part of the essay is concerned with showing that existing alternative theories are in fact more ridiculous than the idea of Father Christmas. I will start by considering the meaning of the question and providing some definitions.

The question is asking whether there really is a person who delivers presents on December 24th each year. The question is inspired by growing speculation in some parts of the population that there is no such person, and that presents arrive by some other means. The chief opposing theory, which is the only one considered in this essay, is that your parents do it.

Various definitions of Father Christmas have been proposed; Rodney Elfman states 'The main man. Don' mess with Santa, he's the boss around here' (Elfman, 1988, p1) while Real Spoilsport holds a very different view 'A fictitious character, traditionally said to deliver presents at Christmas' (Spoilsport, 1953, p.31294). Small Toddler's view is 'Totally brill can't wait' (Toddler, 1993).

So it is apparent that there is an ongoing debate over the existence of Father Christmas. The easiest way to resolve this once and for all would be for somebody to wait up and take a photograph of the person delivering presents. However, since seeing Santa on the night would result in the photographer getting a sack of cinders instead of presents, no researcher has yet volunteered for the task.

So we have no prospect of getting hard evidence, but such circumstantial evidence as there is points strongly in favour of Father Christmas. I will now consider this evidence. Firstly I will evaluate the evidence in favour, and then I will show why the evidence against is inadequate.

First hand accounts from those who are in contact with Father Christmas are available. Of course these could have been made up by those involved, but we should consider the solid reputation of these speakers.

Rudolph has been quoted as saying: 'Of course he exists. Do you think me and the others would whiz round like idiots all night towing a sleigh with nobody in it?' (Rednose, 1975, p48). Of equally good character is Henry the Elf, who said:

> Yeah, I've heard that people say he [Father Christmas] doesn't exist. But in a system of industrialised capitalism there has to be an identifiable owner in charge, otherwise we'd be operating some kind of commie co-operative operation, which we're not. Frankly I don't know where our profits go, but we don't see any of them on the shop floor. Somebody's creaming off the takings, and if it ain't Father Christmas I don't know who else it could be.

(Elf, 1984, p 134)

On a personal level, my mum taught me not to lie, and so she obviously does not lie herself. I remember her telling me about Father Christmas many times, so I am personally convinced.

Further support is given when we consider that in modern homes there is no chimney, or existing chimneys have been blocked by gas or electric fires. It follows that whoever delivers presents must be magic, or else how could the presents get into a locked house?

Now we must consider the main alternative theory, which is that it is your parents who leave out your presents on Christmas Eve.

It is clear that it cannot be your parents. My Mum lives eighty miles away, and has arthritis, so the idea that she travels to my house in the middle of the night and climbs up on the roof (for which she would have to bring a ladder, since mine is locked up) and then drops down the chimney to bring my presents seems much more unlikely than the idea that Father Christmas does it with magic at his disposal.

An argument used against the existence of Father Christmas is that he looks different whenever you see him in different shops or on different TV programmes. It is proposed then that these are people dressed up as Father Christmas, and therefore that the real Father Christmas does not exist.

There is a fundamental flaw in this logic. Just because people dress up as him does not mean he does not exist. You do not have to go to many fancy dress parties to see lots of different looking Hitlers, yet we do not deduce from this that Hitler did not exist.

On weighing up the evidence available, while we cannot conclusively prove that Father Christmas does exist, we can demonstrate that some kind of magic is needed, and that the main alternative theory does not stand up to considered reflection. Upright characters have spoken in favour of his existence, and the fact that some people dress up as him is irrelevant. The evidence clearly leads us to conclude that Father Christmas does really exist.

## References

ELF, H. the (1984) *Memoirs of a Happy Toyshop Worker*, Santaland, Grotto Press.

ELFMAN, R. (1988) *How to Survive in the Toy Industry*, Santaland, Polar Technology Publishing.

REDNOSE, R. (1975) *Santa and Me: The Truth*, Santaland, North Pole Press.

SPOILSPORT, R. (1953) *A Miserable Guide to Christmas*, England, Cynical Press Ltd.

TODDLER, S. (1993) *How to Get Giddy with Excitement at Christmas*, England, Whoopee Press.

# References

BPS (1994) *Guidelines for External Examiners on Undergraduate Psychology Degrees*, Leicester, British Psychological Society/ Association of Heads of Psychology Departments.

BROOK, C. (1987) 'Skills Booklet' in D205 *Changing Britain, Changing Worlds : Geographical Perspectives*, Milton Keynes, The Open University.

COATS, M. (undated) *Open Teaching Toolkit : Learning How to Learn*, Milton Keynes, The Open University.

COLE, S. and HARRIS, P. (undated) *Open Teaching Toolkit : Revision and Examinations*, Milton Keynes, The Open University.

DYER, R. (1989) 'Don't Look Now' in MCROBBIE, A. (ed.) *Zoot Suits and Second-Hand Dresses: An Anthology of Fashion and Music*, Basingstoke, Macmillan Education.

NORTHEDGE, A. (1990) *The Good Study Guide*, Milton Keynes, The Open University.

THE OPEN UNIVERSITY (1994) 'Appendix B: some comments on essay writing' in D309 *Cognitive Psychology, Assignments Booklet*, Milton Keynes, The Open University.

P.N.L. STUDY GUIDES (1992) *How to Write Essays: Suggestions for Teaching Essay Writing*, London, Educational Development Service of the Polytechnic of North London.

RUBIN, D. (1983) *Teaching Reading and Study Skills in Content Areas*, London, Holt, Reinhart and Winston.

SAYERS, J. (1986) *Sexual Contradictions : Psychology, Psychoanalysis, and Feminism*, London, Tavistock.

WALKER, A. (1994) 'Community care policy : from consensus to conflict' in D211 *Social Problems and Social Welfare*, Block 4, *Readings 1: Reconstructing Welfare*, Milton Keynes, The Open University.

# Acknowledgements

Cartoons by Adrian Burrows; reproduced with permission from Robert Barrass (1982) *Students must write*, Andover, Routledge.

Appendix C figure reproduced by permission of the University of North London.